# What it Means
## *to become*
# A Shepherd

# DAG HEWARD-MILLS

*Parchment House*

Unless otherwise stated, all Scripture quotations are taken from the King James Version of the Bible.

Published 2014 by Parchment House

ISBN : 978-1-61395-488-1

Find out more about Dag Heward-Mills at:
Healing Jesus Campaign
Write to:  evangelist@daghewardmills.org
Website:  www.daghewardmills.org
Facebook: Dag Heward-Mills
Twitter:  @EvangelistDag

# *Contents*

# Chapter 1

# What is a Shepherd?

**But when he saw the multitudes, he was moved with compassion on them, because they fainted, and were SCATTERED abroad, as sheep having NO SHEPHERD.**

**Matthew 9:36**

There is no need for us to struggle with the definition of who a shepherd is. A shepherd is a caring loving guide to the sheep. A shepherd is someone whom God has called to look after sheep.

In the bible, God's people are called sheep and He raises up men He calls shepherds to look after these sheep. God does not see us as a collection of snakes, lizards, cats and dogs. No! He sees us as a group of sheep who need love, care and guidance.

**O come, let us worship and bow down: let us kneel before the Lord our maker. For he is our God; and WE ARE THE PEOPLE OF HIS PASTURE, AND THE SHEEP OF HIS HAND.**

**Psalm 95:6-7**

I am writing this book because it is my strong belief that many people can join in taking care of God's sheep. It is time for us to rise up and join the great work of looking after God's people. Being a shepherd is one of the greatest things of all time because our Lord loves the people and sees them as sheep who need care and guidance. Being a shepherd is a very great job. That is why it is the job that was given to apostle Peter, the head of the church. Remember! Jesus told Peter to prove his love by feeding and caring for the sheep. Peter, do you love me? If you love me feed my sheep!

**15 So when they had dined, Jesus saith to Simon Peter, Simon, son of Jonas, lovest thou me more than these?**

He saith unto him, Yea, Lord; thou knowest that I love thee. He saith unto him, Feed my lambs.

16 He saith to him again the second time, Simon, son of Jonas, lovest thou me? He saith unto him, Yea, Lord; thou knowest that I love thee. He saith unto him, Feed my sheep.

17 He saith unto him the third time, Simon, son of Jonas, lovest thou me? Peter was grieved because he said unto him the third time, Lovest thou me? And he said unto him, Lord, thou knowest all things; thou knowest that I love thee. Jesus saith unto him, Feed my sheep

**John 21:15-17**

There are two categories of people in every church: shepherds and sheep. You are either a shepherd or a sheep. A shepherd is basically a pastor. Indeed, in many languages there is not a different word for 'Shepherd' and 'Pastor.' The same word that is used for shepherd is the word that is used for pastor. I prefer using the word shepherd because it helps everyone to understand what the work entails. I prefer using the term 'shepherd' because it is a clearer definition of what a pastor really is. Being a shepherd means that you must see people as sheep and relate with them as such.

There are many strange interpretations of the word 'pastor' and everyone has his own idea of what a pastor should be or do. However, when you say you are a shepherd you immediately know that your job is looking after sheep. Obviously, if you are a shepherd you cannot look after people who do not have sheep-like characteristics and cannot be led, guided, taught or cared for. In the English language, the word pastor is so commonly used to mean 'man of God' or God's representative. Because of this, prophets, apostles, deacons and almost every representative of God is called 'pastor'. A shepherd is a specific type of worker who has time to care, time to love, time to feed and time to gather the sheep.

Notice in the scripture above that the sheep were scattered because there was no shepherd. Sheep are not scattered because there is no prophet. Sheep are not scattered because there is no evangelist or deacon. Sheep are scattered because there is no shepherd. It is my strong belief that many people are called to be shepherds. Many people can give their love, their time, their energy to look after somebody else. I know this because most people become mothers and fathers and have the natural ability to care for their children. Being a shepherd involves so much loving, caring and guiding that the sheep end up calling their shepherds fathers. When someone arises with the anointing of a shepherd, people gather around him because everybody needs love, care and guidance.

Learn to use the word 'shepherd' when describing those who are caring for God's people and feeding them, because that is what they are. When you describe yourself as a shepherd, it helps you to focus on your work as a shepherd. Today, many people who are supposed to be caring loving and guiding the sheep have become secularised people who are more suited to a university than a church.

If you saw a shepherd sitting behind his desk in a bank, you would immediately ask him, 'Where have you left your goats and sheep? What is happening to them? Who is caring for them?' Today, many shepherds have left their goats and sheep and are found in the so-called market places doing something completely different from shepherding. They have despised the honour given to us to care for God's people and to feed them. Don't throw away this book. Shepherding is a very important task. It is God's work. Take it seriously. You can become a shepherd and care for God's children. You can also do something for God!

There was a time we received but it is time for us to give! There was a time we were taught but it is time for us to teach! There was a time that we were led by someone but it is time to lead others! Give up yourself for this noble work of shepherding – loving, caring and teaching people. It is an honour. Even if you are a layperson, you can become a shepherd. Many lay people are in the ministry. You can be one of those honoured lay people who serve God as a shepherd.

If you are in full time ministry, think of yourself as a shepherd rather than a man of God. This will help you to understand your calling better. Flow in the loving, caring, guiding and the teaching gifts of God and you will be a shepherd to God's people. Remember that Jesus loves His sheep very much. He died for us. He must care for us dearly! Anyone who looks after God's sheep has moved directly into the love of God because Jesus loved and died for these sheep.

## Chapter 2

# Why You Can Become a Shepherd

In this chapter, I want to show you that there are many scriptural reasons why I believe you can be a shepherd. I believe that at a point in your Christian development, you can be a shepherd, at least at some level. The Bible teaches from many angles about you being fruitful in ministry. The Word also teaches us that "many" and not "few" are called to the ministry.

> **And he gave some, apostles; and some, prophets; and some, evangelists; and some, pastors [poimen] and teachers; For the perfecting of the saints, for the work of the ministry, for the edifying of the body of Christ:**
>
> **Ephesians 4:11, 12**

The usual interpretation of this Scripture is that God gave special ministerial offices to the Church for three principal reasons:

1. **To perfect the saints.**

2. **To do the work of the ministry.**

3. **To edify the Body of Christ.**

This is true. However, we must be aware that the translators of the Bible added punctuation, which sometimes gives an unfortunate interpretation of the text. When you remove the commas from Ephesians 4:12, it gives a completely different meaning, which I believe is more accurate. Remove the punctuation marks in Ephesians 4:12 and look at what the verse is saying now.

> **And he gave some, apostles; and some, prophets; and some, evangelists; and some, pastors [poimen] and teachers; For the perfecting of the saints for the work of the ministry for the edifying of the body of Christ:**
>
> **Ephesians 4:11, 12**

The scripture is now saying that God gave apostles, prophets, evangelists, pastors and teachers "for the perfecting of the saints for the work of the ministry".

**In other words, these special ministerial offices are given to perfect ordinary saints to enable them (the saints) to do the work of ministry.** What does this mean? This simply means that ordinary saints can do ministry work. It also means that ministry work is not the sole preserve of certain apostles and teachers.

Shepherds can satisfactorily accomplish a large part of the ministry.

When you interpret Ephesians 4:11, 12 this way it puts the responsibility of ministry on all of us and not just on a few special people. This must be the case, because the Bible says many are called!

God never called a few people to do His work. God has always called many more people than have responded.

If you were God and you had a huge task to accomplish—the task of saving the whole world, would you call a few people and send them out? Of course not! You would call as many people as possible and send them out. Unfortunately, few people respond to the call, therefore, few are eventually chosen to serve in the vineyard.

## Is the Call Such a Big Deal?

We have made the call of God to be some mystical experience involving the hearing of voices, seeing of visions, and having of spectacular spiritual experiences. That is an erroneous generalization. Many are "called", but many have not seen visions of Jesus. The Bible teaches us that we are "called" to be saints.

**To all that be in Rome, beloved of God, CALLED TO BE SAINTS...**
**Romans 1:7**

**Unto the church of God which is at Corinth, to them that are sanctified in Christ Jesus, CALLED TO BE SAINTS...**

**1 Corinthians 1:2**

It is the saints who are expected to do the work according to Ephesians 4:12. Now let us be honest. In our calling to be saints, how many of us heard supernatural voices? How many of us have had thunder and lightning frighten us to salvation? How many of us fell down on the way to Damascus? Very few Christians have had such dramatic calls to God.

That however, does not mean that we are not called to be Christians.

All born-again Christians have a supernatural calling on their lives to be saints. It may not be spectacular but it is certainly supernatural. **If you call yourself a Christian, then you have received a call to which you have responded.** I am informing you that without knowing, you have actually heard a call and responded to a divine call.

What was that call? That call was simply a conviction that came upon you about the reality of Jesus Christ. That same conviction led you to give your life to Christ, and made you a born-again Christian.

Sometimes people looking out for the sensational miss the real supernatural move of God. **In the same way that we are called to be Christians, God will call many of us to His service at one level or the other.** You may not be called to a breath-taking level of ministry like Elijah, but it is still a calling!

Look at the ministry of Samuel the prophet. Samuel was in the temple when he received the call of God.

**And the child Samuel ministered unto the Lord before Eli...**

**1 Samuel 3:1**

But notice that Samuel did not know what the call of God was. In fact, he thought it was something very natural, *a man's voice.* Many people are called, but think that because it feels natural, like a thought, an idea or even a conviction, they are not called. Since the call of God is not so different from natural things around us, many just assume they have not been called.

The prophet Samuel went to his father-in-ministry, Eli, thinking that he was calling him. He could not distinguish between a natural human voice and the supernatural voice of God. What does this mean to us?

It means that many times the supernatural is not as dramatic as we expect. If it was that dramatic, Samuel would have immediately known that he was not hearing a human voice.

**...THE LORD CALLED Samuel: and he answered, Here am I. And he ran unto Eli, and said, Here am I; FOR THOU [Eli] CALLEDST ME...**

**1 Samuel 3:4, 5**

It was Eli (his pastor or father-in-ministry) who helped him to recognize the call of God on his life.

## The Allergic Pastor

I have watched many of my church members grow up in the Lord. I have watched God calling them and have seen how many of them did not recognize the call of God on their lives. In fact, some of my best pastors were once allergic to the subject of *being called* to the ministry.

One particular pastor did not want to accept the possibility that the call of God was there. So he developed an allergy to the topic and did not want to discuss it with me at all! He said to me, 'Please, I am allergic to this subject. I don't want to talk about becoming a pastor. I don't want to discuss the idea of becoming a missionary. I am allergic to this subject.' Honestly, I felt rebuked and withdrew because of the 'allergies'. But the Holy Spirit took over and today, he is a successful pastor in full-time ministry, obeying the call of God on his life. You see, you can be called without even knowing it, just like Samuel. This brother was called but did not even know it!

## The Call Is Supernatural

The call to a small ministry is still a call. It is still supernatural. It may not be outwardly impressive, but it is still a call. I have not had the experience of thunder, lightning and heavenly voices calling me to the ministry. But I am just as called as any other minister.

**...but the Lord was not in the wind: and after the wind an earthquake; but the Lord was not in the earthquake: And after the earthquake a fire; but the Lord was not in the fire: and after the fire A STILL SMALL VOICE.**

**1 Kings 19:11, 12**

God often speaks by this still small voice. It was the still small voice of conviction that brought me into the ministry. I have just had a quiet conviction. It is that conviction that I have followed up until this time.

## Be Open to the Call

Pastors ought to encourage their members to be open to the call. This will release many more Christians into useful ministry. **It is this secret of releasing many people into the ministry that brings about church growth.** One man can do very little, but many people can do a great deal. One pastor can probably remember the names of only one hundred and fifty people in his church.

**How can one man, who does not even know the names and problems of most of the people in his church, effectively pastor thousands of people?** That is why we need the help of many shepherds.

I am always encouraging everyone to be open to the call to the ministry. In fact, if you ask my congregation whether they are called or not, most of them will respond, "I believe I am called!" The Bible said that many are called and not a few.

Samuel stayed in the temple and was able to hear the call of God. **Serious Christians, who spend a lot of time in church doing the work of the ministry, are likely to hear the call of God.** I also think that Christians who spend time at clubs, parties and the like do not hear the voice of God. Even if they are called, they will not be able to hear it because of the other distractions in their lives.

## Who Is Ordained?

We all quote this famous verse of Scripture on prayer.

**Whatsoever ye shall ask of the Father in my name, he may give it you.**
**John 15:16b**

We believe that whatever we ask the Father, He will give it to us. In fact, we have great confidence that this scripture applies to all Christians and not just to the apostles. However, what does the first part of that verse say? It says,

**...I HAVE CHOSEN YOU, AND ORDAINED YOU, that ye should go and bring forth fruit, and that your fruit should remain...**
**John 15:16**

Is this ordination and choosing not the same thing as a calling? It certainly is! If you believe that God, the Father will hear all of our prayers then we must believe that God has chosen and ordained all of us to go and bear fruit. This leaves no one out, including you. **This means that Christian doctors, lawyers and businessmen are also ordained ministers who are expected to bear much fruit.** What is the fruit that he is talking about? The fruit of souls brought to the Lord. The fruit of people being established in the Lord. Who does that? A shepherd.

If you expect God to answer all of your prayers, you must first bear much fruit. **Many people are fainting and are being**

10

scattered because there are not enough shepherds. There are a lot of big-time men of God but there are not enough shepherds.

Let me now show you ten reasons why I think every Christian can do the work of a shepherd.

## Why Every Christian Can Become a Shepherd

**1. To become a shepherd, all you need is a desire.**

The Bible says if anyone has the desire to become a bishop, he has desired a good thing. Let us not deviate from the Word of God.

> **This is a true saying, if a man desire the OFFICE OF A BISHOP, he desireth a good work.**
>
> **1 Timothy 3:1**

The Word is telling us here that in order to become a bishop all we need is a desire. Let it be clear that a bishop is simply a shepherd or pastor.

The Greek word translated bishop is episkopos, which means an overseer of God's people.

Apostle Paul's vision was to enjoin more people to do God's work. He therefore asked Timothy to look out for people with a desire to be involved in ministry. After locating people who had a desire to do the work, Paul instructed Timothy to ensure that they were of honourable reputation. **All the qualities that Paul asked Timothy to look for were matters of character and not talent, ability or anointing.**

Paul was making it very easy for anyone to become a shepherd. All you needed to do was to have a desire and an unquestionable character. Pastors, look out for people who have a desire for God's work and who have an honest and faithful character. **If that is what the Bible teaches us to look out for, then we cannot be more spiritual than God.**

Some of my most fruitful pastors do not look outwardly anointed or talented. But, because God was looking for their faithfulness and integrity they have grown to be very successful in ministry.

## 2. Becoming a shepherd is a natural stage of development.

**FOR WHEN FOR THE TIME YE OUGHT TO BE TEACHERS, ye have need that one teach you again which be the first principles of the oracles of God; and are become such as have need of milk, and not of strong meat.**

**Hebrews 5:12**

When Paul wrote to the Hebrew Christians, he made it clear that he was disappointed in the fact that when they should have been teachers themselves, they still needed instruction. He talks about a time when you need to be a teacher yourself.

**There is a time in every Christian's life when he must be able to teach.** This is a natural stage of development. It does not require any special or spectacular experience with God to be able to teach. **Teaching is the principal duty of a good shepherd.** Teaching is the same as feeding the sheep.

I have found out that when Christians do not develop normally into shepherds they often turn into something bad. A time comes when some of the church members know exactly what the pastor is going to preach. They know how he will begin the message and how it will end. They heard the same message two years ago. They end up becoming critical.

In the medical field, when a person has more food than he uses the food is converted into fat and the person becomes obese. Obesity is a dangerous disease that can kill you. It is simply caused by being overfed and under-exercised. **That is the problem of many Christians; they have nothing to do with the knowledge that is being imparted to them Sunday after Sunday.** They never use the knowledge they have. They never feed anyone. They never minister to anyone. They then become a danger to themselves!

A dangerous sign that you should look out for in your own life is when you become full of criticism. People who criticize a lot are often not involved in the work of God.

I remember one critical friend. He had many comments to make about different men of God. However, he himself did not do much in the ministry and was more like a commentator. Beware of commentating Christians! They fill your mind with poison!

Let's all grow up naturally, and begin to teach when we need to teach and shepherd when we need to shepherd. Pastors, encourage your members to become shepherds and feeders of sheep under you. Allow them to become solvers of problems and helpers of the weak. Everyone can do it!

I remember a doctor colleague whose wife went into the labour ward to deliver a baby. Unfortunately, the woman was permitted to labour too long and the baby became distressed (short of oxygen). Eventually the doctors took a decision to operate on the lady and she gave birth to a child who had brain damage. I never saw this child! About five or six years later, I met someone who had visited this lady and I asked about the child: "How is the child doing?"

She said, "Oh pastor. It's a pathetic story. This child is six years old and cannot talk or move. He sits in a chair and defecates and urinates all over himself. He is growing into a boy but has no control whatsoever of any of these functions!"

She said to me, "It's a sorry sight. Because when a baby messes up, it's quite different from when a grown boy does the same thing!"

She went on, "What an embarrassment it is to the parents. And how difficult it is for them to cope with the situation."

As I reflected on this story, the Spirit of the Lord showed me how similar the condition of this child was to many Christians. When they should be performing certain functions naturally, they still need to be carried about, fed and cleaned by someone else.

Spiritually, that is also a pathetic situation! A situation of no growth and no development.

Recently I had a call from a young man. I got to know this young man about seven years ago, when he was just nineteen years old. At that time he was a student, but hadn't taken his education seriously. I said to him, "You have to take your education seriously!"

I even tried to help him to continue his schooling. I even promised, "I will pay for every single one of your books, if only you will go to school."

After I made that promise, I did not see this young man for a long while. He just wasn't interested in his studies. The next time I saw him was at a family funeral. When I saw him, I wondered what he was up to. I didn't speak to him but then out of the blue, seven years later this young man gave me a phone call.

"Hullo!"

"Yes," I answered. He mentioned his name. "Oh, I see. It's been a long time. What can I do for you?"

It was his birthday. He told me his story and said, "Things are difficult for me now. I am twenty-six years old and I have no man to help me now."

I said, "I see. What can I do for you?"

"Since I have no one to help me now I wanted to ask you if you could start helping me. And if I could be coming to you for pocket money."

"Pocket money!" I exclaimed.

This was a twenty-six year old man who did not work but wanted to collect pocket money from me on a regular basis. What he had failed to realize was that there is a time you can receive pocket money and there is a time you must work. In every sphere of life, you are expected to develop and grow into the next stage. If you fail to do so you will become an anomaly in society.

I said to this young man, "Come and see me in my office."

When he came I told him, "The days of collecting pocket money like a child are over. You must work now! Nobody is going to give you pocket money at this stage of your life. We can help you go to school or help you get a job, but you cannot expect regular handouts from me."

You must develop into a teacher or shepherd that feeds God's people. You are expected to develop and become a feeder according to Hebrews 5:12. If you fail to do this you will become an awkward, critical, malformed, and retarded Christian.

3. **There is a great need for shepherds.**

**But when he saw the multitudes, he was moved with compassion on them, because they fainted, and were scattered abroad, as sheep having no shepherd.**
**Matthew 9:36**

In this Scripture, Jesus makes it clear that people are fainting and being harassed because there is no shepherd.

When I was growing up as a Christian, I learnt a lot by talking to senior Christians (who were like shepherds to me). Every difficult question I had, I directed it to them. They were easily accessible people I could talk to. When I had difficult questions like, "Who created God?" "Why did Jesus have to die?" and "Who was Cain's wife?" I always had somebody to ask.

**Today, in some of the big churches, pastors are almost unavailable because the reality is that one man cannot attend to the personal needs of so many thousands of people.** Yes, he can preach to thousands, but he cannot personally talk to thousands. He cannot answer questions and spend time with the needy thousands. He is likely to have a break down if he tries to.

I believe in preaching to thousands from the pulpit, but I believe in having shepherds on the ground that minister one-on-one to the multitudes. Although I preach to thousands, I still enjoy attending to the personal needs of as many of the flock as I can.

When you decide to become a shepherd, the lives of certain people will be changed forever. If you do not become a shepherd, perhaps many lives will never become stable in Christ. When you, an ordinary Christian, decide to become a shepherd (someone with the Word of God and solutions), people will begin to gather around you. It is then that you will minister to them Living Water.

## 4. God's people are scattered without a shepherd.

**And they were scattered, because there is no shepherd: and they became meat to all the beasts of the field, when they were scattered.**

**Ezekiel 34:5**

I remember when I was in Achimota School in Accra, Ghana, there was no Scripture Union (SU) fellowship on the western compound. You see, Achimota School, being one of the largest schools in Ghana, had two compounds, the east and the west.

There was a vibrant SU fellowship on the eastern compound but none on the west. I took it upon myself to begin a fellowship on the western compound. After a while, there was a gathering of the western compound SU members into the western assembly hall. This western SU fellowship became so dynamic that some easterners even began to walk to the west to attend these meetings.

What am I saying? The SU members (God's sheep) were scattered on the west when there was no shepherd. But with the rising up of a shepherd God's people began to gather and were blessed.

The devil wants us to be scattered because he knows that he can get the sheep when they are alone.

**When the sheep are together in a group they are safer and the devil knows it!** That is why Satan does not want you to be a shepherd. Satan wants the sheep to be scattered. The devil wants to prevent you from becoming a shepherd because it is the shepherd who will gather the sheep. That is why the devil has blinded the eyes of many pastors preventing them from seeing the potential shepherds amongst the congregation who could help greatly in the work.

## 5.  Become a shepherd in order to fulfil the great commission.

Jesus' last words to his disciples on top of a lonely hill were, **"Go ye... and make disciples...teaching them..."**

Traditionally, we think of the Great Commission as an evangelistic command. Yet when you study the instructions of our Lord very carefully, you will realize that the Great Commission is also a shepherdorial commission. It is a pastoral commission. It is a mandate for shepherds to move out and to begin to teach the Word of God. Christian friend, it is up to you and I to go out there and fulfil the Great Commission.

The evangelist has an anointing to preach and to lead people to Christ. That was the first instruction Jesus gave to Peter; come and I will make you fishers of men.

His last words added something to the first words—the teaching element.

I once read about a famous evangelist who was holding mammoth crusades in every city of the world. One day this evangelist returned to one of the cities where he had held a crusade and did a survey of all the people who had taken decisions for Christ during his last crusade. The result of his survey was frightening. It showed that only 5% of the converts of his last massive crusade were still Christians.

I don't think the evangelist was very happy about these results. The poor results led him to establish a strong follow-up ministry. You see, the evangelists' preaching alone does not fulfil the Great Commission. There is a need for shepherds to rise up to finish his work.

A cell leader is a shepherd. A pastor is a shepherd. A bishop is a shepherd. It is the same ministry operating at different levels. You must decide to develop into a shepherd so that you can help to fulfill the Great Commission. Jesus said; go and teach them because they (the sheep) need shepherds. After you have received for so many years, it is time for you to give.

Teaching builds people. Teaching builds churches. Teaching fulfils the Great Commission.

## 6. Become a shepherd so that you can obtain a good degree.

I went to the university in 1982 and finished in 1989 with a degree in medicine and surgery. That degree is intended to help me for the rest of my life on this earth. Many Christians do not know about the existence of a heavenly degree. I can assure you that just as a university degree will guarantee you forty or so years of comfortable living on this earth, a good heavenly degree will guarantee an eternity of comfort and blessings.

Make no mistake my friend. God is not blind! God is not a fool! God is not mocked! Whatever you sow on earth you will reap.

Paul said that if anyone used the office of a deacon (which is a church helper or a shepherd), he would have a good degree in heaven.

**For they that have used the office of a deacon well purchase to themselves A GOOD DEGREE, and great boldness in the faith...**
**1 Timothy 3:13**

God wants all of us to have this degree. Some of you might not have earthly degrees but you can obtain a heavenly one when you function as a shepherd.

If you have been a good shepherd you can be bold when you think about going to Heaven. Your degree will help you up there!

## 7. Become a shepherd so that you can combine material and spiritual progress

**But godliness with contentment is great gain.**
**1 Timothy 6:6**

You may never enter into full-time ministry. You may pursue a career and acquire all the houses and cars you want. There is nothing wrong with that.

Understand that God is not against your material prosperity. All that the Bible is saying here is that, if you are able to add onto your material blessings, godliness or spiritual blessings then you are truly blessed.

While in the medical school, I trained to become a doctor. But I didn't just become a medical doctor. I started a church when I was in my fourth year and by the time I qualified with my medical degree, I was also an experienced minister of the gospel. I had a material and a spiritual degree. I had them both! I did not have one without the other. I wasn't a spiritually bankrupt doctor.

I was a doctor who was a shepherd as well. Many have one but not the other. Strive to have both and not just one. It is a greater blessing (great gain) to have both. This is what the Bible means **by godliness and contentment. In my case, the "godliness" was in becoming a pastor and the "contentment" was in becoming a doctor.** You can have that too! You can be a businessman and at the same time a minister of God's sheep! You can get all of the money you desire and at the same time fulfil your God-given ministry of being a shepherd.

**Most of the pastors in my denomination are lay pastors.** They work very hard in the secular world, and there is nothing wrong with that. Some of them are millionaires and yet they pastor God's sheep as well. Isn't that a blessing? What more could you ask for?

**8. Become a shepherd because people are hungry for the truth.**

People have a hunger in their spirits that can only be satisfied by the Word of God.

**...should not the shepherds feed the flocks?**

**Ezekiel 34:2**

I remember when I was a young Christian; I would always have biblical discussions with Christian leaders. That helped me a lot in my spiritual development. Let's ask ourselves; when the pastor preaches on one topic how does he meet the needs of a thousand different people at the same time? That is why we need shepherds of all degrees who will feed the sheep at every level.

## The Disastrous Fast

Some sheep need attention that a particular pastor may not be able to give. There is a need for all kinds of shepherds. God needs lady shepherds to do His work as well. Sometimes when a male shepherd tries to help a female sheep in the "mud", he may get his feet dirty. Perhaps a female shepherd may be more suitable than a male one.

I remember a lady who came to see us in the church office. She had a problem with fornication and adultery. I asked, "What have you been doing about this problem?"

She said, "So-and-so evangelist came to our church to preach and minister deliverance. Afterwards he called and asked me to come for further deliverance at his home church."

"Did you go?" I asked.

She said, "Yes."

"What did he tell you at his home church?" I inquired.

"He said that he had discerned by the Spirit that I needed extra counselling and deliverance. So, he decided to fast with me for seven days," she replied.

"Did you get delivered after the seven days?" I queried.

"I hope so!" She said.

"At the end of the seven day fast, when we were praying together in his house, we fornicated."

She continued, "It happened several times."

20

Please notice that the pastor was so kind as to actually fast for seven days with this sheep who needed counselling and deliverance. Not all pastors would lay aside their stomachs to help a sheep in need. Unfortunately, his help ended up in disaster. Perhaps a lady pastor or shepherd would have been a better person to fast and counsel with this sheep.

*Make no mistake about this, it is not only a physical hunger that people have, they also have a spiritual hunger.* Even in Europe and America, this same spiritual hunger leads them to go after the occult and witchcraft.

## 9. Become a shepherd because many people are spiritually hungry.

Once while in Geneva I decided to attend a church service in a very large and old building. I wanted to see how the churches in the land were faring. In the church were eight old men and women. You could see that they didn't have much more than a few years to live. There was no young person in the church. The church building was virtually empty!

Most Swiss people have virtually stopped going to church. Many of them no longer believe in God. Yet, they still have a spiritual hunger - a great spiritual need. When I saw a large occult/witchcraft shop, a few blocks down the road, I was not surprised.

Switzerland has a very high number of such cults and witchcraft activities. The reason for the multiplication of false cults and witchcraft is obvious. The spiritual vacuum has to be filled by something!

Since there are no shepherds, the devil is having a field day in such places. The Bible says in Matthew 9:36, "He was moved with compassion... because they fainted... as sheep having no shepherd."

## 10. Become a shepherd because people need to be visited and strengthened.

One thing that cannot be replaced by any other is a visit from your pastor. It is a blessing for a shepherd to come to your house. Remember, Jesus visited the earth for only three years and the earth has never been the same. People need to be visited.

A visit is different from a phone call. A visit is different from a powerful ministration of the Word in church. The sheep need to know that they have not been forgotten. They need to know that someone knows where they are. God needs more shepherds to go forth and strengthen the sheep. The Bible says that love never fails. When the sheep are visited, they feel that the pastor genuinely loves them.

You may be a mature and successful Christian who has a lot within you that can strengthen other people. Make the time to be a shepherd who visits somebody.

**Ye have scattered my flock, and driven them away, and have not visited them...**

**Jeremiah 23:2**

Instead of watching useless films on television and sleeping for twelve hours, get out of your house and minister to someone. Be the shepherd you are called to be!

## Do You Know Whether You Are Called?

Do you know whether you are called? That is a good question. **I cannot tell whether you are called by looking at your nice face.** No one can tell whether you are called by listening to you speak. As you do the work, you will begin to realize the talents and anointing within you.

I believe in the calling of a shepherd. Remember, God has given every one of us talents, however some people feel that what they have is so small that it is not important. God will judge you for doing nothing. God will not judge you only because you are immoral or wicked but also because you are doing nothing to help the Kingdom! Many times Jesus illustrated that doing nothing in certain circumstances is tantamount to being wicked.

If you are not in a church that allows people to rise up and become shepherds, perhaps you should move out to where you can be more fruitful.

# *Chapter 3*

# How to Become a Shepherd

Ⅰn this chapter, I want to lay out five important conditions for anyone in the church to become a shepherd.

## Five Important Conditions for Becoming a Shepherd

### 1.  A shepherd must have a desire.

The first condition is simple – *you must have a desire.*

Timothy was pastoring a large church and probably had the task of bringing up future pastors and leaders. He must have sent an SOS message to Apostle Paul for guidance in this matter. It was very significant that Paul wrote back and laid out very clearly the conditions for anyone to become a pastor in Timothy's church.

> **This is a true saying, If a man DESIRE the office of a bishop, he DESIRETH a good work.**
>
> **1 Timothy 3:1**

The first thing he said was that if anyone has a desire for God's work, he *desires* a good thing. In other words, it is a good thing for members in the church to desire and aspire to become pastors.

Let's be honest. **Why shouldn't members of the church aspire to the highest possible office in the church structure? In the local church, the highest possible office is that of the pastor.**

### I Never Had a Desire to Clean Toilets

I remember years ago, as I walked up and down the corridors of different hospitals, I never once remember having the desire to be a hospital cleaner, laboratory man, or even a technician. I only had a desire for the highest possible position in the hospital that is the position of a *doctor*. When someone walks into a bank, he would naturally aspire to become a *bank manager*.

Why is it that people in the church are not taught to aspire for the highest position in the church? It is biblical to desire the highest office in the church.

Do not desire just to be an usher. Do not desire just to sing in the choir. Desire to be a pastor! I used to play the drums and the organ in church. But I wanted to go as high as I could. The highest position in the church is not the organist. I am not talking about replacing the senior pastor. I am not talking about displacing the people above you. I am talking about rising into responsible and fruitful positions within the church.

Dear ministers of God, if you teach your people that they can also be shepherds, they will believe it and rise up to the occasion. Here again, I am not talking about anybody leaving their job, I'm talking about becoming a shepherd. The church does not have an infinite amount of money, and therefore cannot employ an infinite number of people. (Actually, that is why many churches are broke; because they employ far too many people).

## Even the Tax Collector Was Surprised!

Recently, when the tax office investigated our church, they were surprised to find such a small number of people employed by the church. They asked for the list of pastors in the church. We gave them a long list. However, they did not believe that most of our pastors were gainfully employed elsewhere.

Our chief accountant told them, "This one works in the bank. And this one is an army officer. This one is a nurse..." But they still didn't believe us. They promised to investigate all of these pastors' work places to verify whether we were telling the truth.

Some pastors unfortunately criticize and spread bad stories about sister churches. This keeps them in darkness. Instead of learning the secrets that have made others great, they want to bring their brothers down.

I do not criticize other churches. I think all churches have a role to play. I learn from all successful churches around me, including those in my own city. I read all of the books written by pastors from my own city and I learn from them instead of fighting them. If somebody has a secret that I do not have, why shouldn't I learn from him?

Pastors, look for men and women who have a genuine desire to do God's work. You see, people having a desire or interest in the ministry is supernatural. It may not be a sensational experience but in a sense it is a burden put there by God. I believe that the desire for ministry is a symptom of a divine call within.

## 2. A shepherd must have a divine call.

You must have a divine call. The ministry is not a human institution. The Bible makes it clear that you need to have a divine call to serve in a certain capacity.

> **And no man taketh this honour unto himself, but he that is CALLED OF GOD, as was Aaron.**
>
> **Hebrews 5:4**

Whenever I interview people who want to be in the ministry, I ask them if they believe they have a call of God on their lives. **Without the conviction of a call you cannot be a pastor.** Many people do not even know what it means to have a divine call. They don't know whether they are called or not!

**I believe that one of the principal manifestations of a divine call is a supernatural desire and interest in the work of the ministry.** Paul had a supernatural interest for the salvation of all men, including the Jews.

> **Brethren, MY HEART'S DESIRE and prayer to God for Israel is, that they might be saved.**
>
> **Romans 10:1**

Paul had this desire in him and it was this desire that was translated into practical ministry time and time again. Christian friend, don't take the call of God lightly. **You could pay with your life for disobeying the divine call.**

I have always had the desire to help God's people and to prevent God's sheep from falling away from the fold. One of my favourite songs begins like this, *"Father, help your children"*. That desire in me is a manifestation of a divine call to the pastoral office.

## The Sixteen-Year Old Shepherd

I've been a shepherd or pastor since I was sixteen years old in secondary school. I didn't call myself "pastor" then, but it was easy to see that I was called to be a pastor. I would draw up lists of the Scripture Union members who were in the fellowship and pray for them. I would mention each and every name and pray for them daily. I had long lists of names of over a hundred people. Mind you, no one was paying me to do this!

When it was time to go on holidays, I would draw maps to everyone's house and would visit them during the vacation. Was that not a sixteen-year old pastor visiting his sheep? It certainly was! **You see, the supernatural desire to do God's work is often a manifestation of a divine call.** I believe that is why Paul asked Timothy to look for the desire and didn't even mention the call. The desire is a manifestation of a divine call.

Dear pastors, look out for people with the desire for the work. Most people don't know what a call is. They certainly do understand when they have a desire.

I want to emphasize here that it is important to respond to the call of God on your life. If you were standing downstairs and your boss called for you from upstairs, wouldn't you run to him? What do you think would happen if you ignored his calls when he knew that you could hear him? You might lose your job. It is a different thing if you do not know that you have been called. If you do know that God is calling you and refuse, you might be endangering your very life.

3. **A shepherd must have a willing commitment**

   **...necessity is laid upon me; yea, woe is unto me, if I preach not the gospel! FOR IF I DO THIS THING**

27

**WILLINGLY, I have a reward: but if against my will, a dispensation of the gospel is committed unto me.**

**1 Corinthians 9:16, 17**

There must be a willing commitment to obey the call of God on your life. Some people know that they are called! They even have a desire to do the work, yet you do not see any commitment in them.

**...Then said I, Here am I; SEND ME.**

**Isaiah 6:8**

Notice that Isaiah didn't say, "Here am I, *SEND HIM!*" He said, "Here am I, send me!" That is the true sign of commitment for any Christian.

## Pilot or Pastor?

For instance, I have always had the desire to be a pilot and to fly a plane. Because of that, when I travel I have often gone into the cockpit of the plane. I have even stayed in the cockpit during takeoff and landing. But beyond this, I have made no effort to become a pilot. I am more of an admirer of pilots. I am not serious about becoming a pilot, otherwise, I would have taken some other steps by now.

It is the same thing for some people who claim to be called into the ministry. They make no efforts to be available or involved in day-to-day church life. There is no extra commitment or willing sacrifice.

**I take no notice of such people when they tell me that Jesus has appeared to them, calling them to the ministry.** They are no nearer the ministry, than I am to the moon!

Samuel was available in the temple when he heard the call of God and responded.

**...Then Samuel answered, Speak; for THY SERVANT HEARETH.**

**1 Samuel 3:10**

28

### 4. A shepherd must have a godly character.

There is no substitute for godliness and a good character. Your faithfulness is the cornerstone of your character.

When I started out in ministry, I was initially impressed by flamboyant and well-spoken people. I thought that was the call of God. As the years have passed, I have absolutely no confidence in the outward and impressive show. I have found that there are people who are quiet, not impressive, but faithful in character. These people are to be preferred one hundred times more than outwardly impressive pastors.

## Fire Brings out the Serpent Character

That is why your Bible school certificate, your nice dressing or the ability to sing may not earn you a position in the pastorate. You simply have to be around long enough for us to know you and what you are made out of. **Even with stringent character filters, we still have some sticks turning out to be snakes.**

Whenever there is a test of some sort, you will notice some of your firewood sticks turn into snakes. Remember the incident when Paul was gathering some sticks to light a fire. When he lit the fire, a snake jumped out from among the sticks.

**As the senior pastor, beware of people whom you feel under pressure to promote.** Beware of people whom you feel under pressure to show appreciation. Beware of people whom you feel under pressure to increase their salaries. Such people will not be satisfied anyway with your show of appreciation.

There is only one qualification for people who want to join the pastoral team – *they have to stay around long enough*. They have to "company" around long enough for time and the elements to test them.

Pastors, do not just accept impressive ministers from other churches to work with you. It could be the mistake of your life. Am I speaking a biblical truth or am I speaking my mind? When the apostles had to choose a replacement for Judas, what did they say? Whom did they choose?

What did they do? They didn't choose the best worship leader or the most charismatic speaker. No! They chose a tested and tried person.

**Wherefore of these men which have COMPANIED WITH US all the time that the Lord Jesus went in and out among us, Beginning from the baptism of John, unto that same day that he was taken up from us, must one be ordained to be a witness with us of his resurrection.**

**Acts 1:21, 22**

I take no notice of sweet words showered on me by some job-seekers. All I say in my mind is, "I commend you to God and to time." If with the passage of time, your character remains proper, then and only then will I believe those sweet words. The breakup of many churches and the painful conflicts in many ministries are because people are not abiding by biblical rules for pastoral selection.

Someone cannot be a pastor unless you know his character. **You can never know someone's character unless you have known him for some years.** There are many gifted people who have a lot of skeletons in their wardrobe. Samson operated in the gift of working of miracles. At the same time he had a major problem with fornication and adultery.

## The Untested Pastor

I remember a pastor who came along to work in our church for a while. I have never seen someone so talented and anointed in ministry. One day I found out that he was having the young ladies in the church to cut his fingernails and toenails in his apartment. So I asked him, "Do you think that it is helpful as a young and unmarried man to have ladies doting over you and cutting your nails?"

30

To my surprise he answered, "Yes I do! It saves me time."

I went on and warned him to be careful. Not long after that, one of the young ladies in church approached me, and told me how this pastor had had sex with her on several different occasions. I had known this preacher just by watching him minister, but had not known him for a long length of time. If I had known of all his problems, I would have never welcomed him into my church.

One night after holding a crusade I called this pastor to sit in my car with me because I wanted to talk with him. As we talked, I questioned him about his relationship with the ladies but he was defiant. Suddenly I smelt the unmistakable scent of alcohol. I said, "You have been drinking!"

He smiled, "No pastor!"

You see this gifted pastor had multiple problems: he was a fornicator, drunkard, smoker and a liar. Irrespective of all this, he was beautifully anointed to preach and lead worship. Pastors, save yourselves from the pain of bringing in untested leaders. **Do not spoil the work you have built by bringing in rebels from outside to fill key positions.**

The whole of 1 Timothy 3 is a catalogue of character qualifications for every serious minded minister. Read it for yourselves. You will never read anything about a bishop or pastor having to be anointed or gifted. There is no instruction that a pastor must be talented or charming (in fact, be careful of "charming" pastors). The nearest thing to a gift in the catalogue of character qualifications is where it says a bishop must be apt to teach (1 Timothy 3:2). That only means he that must be able to share the Word of God effectively.

## 5. The wife of a shepherd must be qualified for ministry.

The Bible continues to talk about the characters of the wives of the pastors. Not only is a pastor's character important, but also the character of his wife. Even the character of the pastor's wife has a bearing on his ministry. A Bible school certificate is not the only qualification for the ministry. Certainly not! That is why our Bible school involves a long enough period where we can get to know the disposition of students.

It may not be such a fast and easy way of raising up pastors but it sure is a safer, stronger and more stable way of doing things. After all, that is God's way and none of us can be wiser than God.

Watch out for these qualifications in shepherds.

# Thirty Pauline Qualifications for Shepherds

1. *Blameless in conduct* (Greek - anepileptos) (1 Timothy 3:2; 5:7; 6:14.)

2. *Husband of one wife* i.e., no polygamist. One could be a bishop without a wife, as Paul, (1 Corinthians 9:5).

3. *Vigilant* (Greek - nephalios), drinking no wine; sober. Translated vigilant (1 Timothy 3:2); and sober, (1 Timothy 3:11; Titus 2:2).

4. *Sober* (Greek - sophron), of sound mind; discreet; prudent; moderate; self-controlled; temperate. Translated sober (1 Timothy 3:2; Titus 1:8); temperate (Titus 2:2); and discreet (Titus 2:5).

5. *Of good behaviour,* (Greek - kosmios), (1 Timothy 2:9.)

6. *Given to hospitality* (Greek - philozenon) lover of strangers, (Titus 1:8; 1 Peter 4:9; Romans 12:13).

7. *Apt to teach* (Greek - didaktikos) capable of teaching, (2 Timothy 2:24).

8. *Not given to wine* (Greek - paroinos) a winebibber (Titus 1:7).

9. *No striker* (Greek - plektes) not quarrelsome; one not ready to strike back at those who displease him; no persecutor of those who differ with him, (Titus 1:7).

10. *Not greedy for filthy lucre* (Greek - aischrokerde) not desirous of base gain; not using wrong methods to raise money to increase his own income, (1 Timothy 3:3, 8; Titus 1:7).

11. *Patient* (Greek-epieikes) meek and gentle, (1Timothy 3:3, Philippians 4:5).

12. *Not a brawler* (Greek - amachos) not contentious, but quiet and peaceable. (Titus 3:2).

13. *Not covetous* (Greek - aphilarguros) not a lover of money; not desiring the office for the sake of personal gain, (Hebrews 13:5; Luke 12:15).

14. *Ruler of his own house*, not by hardness and tyranny but with honesty, (1 Timothy 3:4).

15. *Not a novice* (Greek - neophuton) new convert to the faith, (1 Timothy 3:6).

16. *Of a good report from outsiders* (1 Timothy 3:7).

## More Qualifications for Shepherds and Their Wives

17. *Grave* (1 Timothy 3:8) (Greek - semnos). Translated grave (1 Timothy 3:4; Titus 2:2) and honest (Philippians 4:8).

18. *Not double tongued* (1 Timothy 3:8) (Greek—dilogos) liars; saying different things to different persons on the same subject. Only used once in the Bible.

19. *Not given to much wine* (1 Timothy 3:8) even unfermented (in the cluster; Is 65:8).

20. *Not greedy of filthy lucre* (1 Timothy 3:8).

21. *Holding the mystery of the faith in a pure conscience* (1 Timothy 3:9). They must maintain a good conscience and be able demonstrate the mysterious power of faith, (Mark 9:23; 11:22-24; 16:17, 18).

22. *Let them be proved* (1 Timothy 3:1). The same as not a new convert in 1 Timothy 3:6. Let them be tested and proved worthy of the office, and able to keep themselves from being lifted up in pride and falling in the same manner Satan did.

23. *Blameless* (Greek - anegkletos) (1 Timothy 3:10. Translated blameless, (1 Timothy 3:10; 1 Corinthians 1:8; Titus 1:6-7) and unreprovable, (Colossians 1:22). They must be free from evil and reproach.

24. *Their wives must meet certain qualifications* (1 Timothy 3:11).

25. Each, the husband of one wife (1 Timothy 3:12) No polygamist.

26. *Each, the ruler of his own house* (1 Timothy 3:12), as required of bishops (1 Timothy 3:4, 5).

27. *Grave* (1 Timothy 3:11).

28. *Not slanderers* (1 Timothy 3:11) (Greek - diabolos), devils.

29. *Sober* (1 Timothy 3:11), (Greek - nephalios) not drinkers of wine.

30. *Faithful in all things* (1 Timothy 3:11). These qualifications apply to wives of bishops, deacons, deaconesses, and Christian women in general.

## Chapter 4

# How I Discovered the Ministry of a Shepherd

Ihave experienced two worlds of ministry—full-time ministry and lay ministry. Most pastors are only aware of the existence of the full-time dimension of ministry. In this book, my intention is to help you to discover the reality of lay people doing the work of ministry.

**A lay shepherd is someone who maintains his secular job and yet is active in the ministry of the Lord Jesus.** A full-time minister is someone who has abandoned his secular job to concentrate fully on the ministry. Many ministers who are in full-time ministry are not comfortable with the idea of lay people participating in the ministry. This is because they want to maintain the ministry as the exclusive preserve of a few "called" men of God.

*Some full-time ministers do not want to accept the reality that lay people are capable of making a substantial (non-financial) contribution to ministry.* Many full-time ministers are happy to maintain their lay people as mere financial supporters. They think, "After all, if you can do the job I'm doing, what makes me special?" Pastors want to feel special as they perform their exclusive ministerial duties. "Why should a lay person do what I do?" they say. "What makes me (the pastor) different if he can do the things I do?" they ask.

Other ministers are not convinced that lay people can do the work of the ministry. I have had pastors ask me, "Will they have time to attend to the needs of the flock?", "Can they handle emergencies?" "Can they minister powerfully the way we do?"

The answers to these are very simple - a resounding YES! I have been in the lay ministry for many years and have found it to be practically possible.

*The lay ministry is the key to church growth.* Churches in this world which have experienced phenomenal growth have all employed the principle of using lay people for the ministry. I believe that it is the key to fulfilling the Great Commission. There is no way we are going to win this world with just a few priests and pastors. Everyone must get involved. Many people must get involved at a higher ministerial level. There must be a revival of the lay ministry in the church.

**Full-time pastors must be secure in their positions in order to encourage lay people to get involved.** There is nothing mystical about the ministry! There are pastors who want the ministry to be shrouded in mystery so that their members feel dependent on them.

In this book, I intend to demystify the art of shepherding and pastoring people. It is something that many can get involved with. What a blessing it is for many other people to discover that they can be useful in the ministry. What a blessing for the pastor when he discovers that the contributions of lay shepherds make his church grow.

I am not saying that there is no need for full-time ministers. I myself am a full-time minister today. There is a great need for certain people to be one hundred percent involved in ministry work. There are things that only full-time ministers can do.

## I Was a Shepherd

At the age of about fifteen, in secondary school, I met the Lord. From the day I gave my life to Christ, I became very active in ministry. I was involved in soul winning and following up converts. I was also involved in singing and playing musical instruments for the Lord.

In the first phase of my Christian life, I was not a traditional Sunday morning church attendee. In fact, I hardly went to church on Sundays. **My Christian life was so active from Monday to Saturday that I ended up resting on Sundays!** Mondays and Wednesdays I had a prayer meeting and Bible study. On Tuesdays and Thursdays I had music rehearsals. On Fridays we had fasting and prayer meetings. And then on Saturdays we would have a retreat from ten in the morning until six in the evening.

Whilst I was involved in these activities I never gave up my schooling. I completed my 'O' levels and passed with a distinction - I had seven one's (one is the highest mark of distinction). That was a great accomplishment by any standards. In my 'A' levels I topped my class and was one of the only people from my school admitted into the medical school. Throughout this period, I was fully involved in ministry. I preached! I won souls! I visited people in their homes! I counselled many people! I fasted and prayed! At one point, I fasted so much that I became as thin as a rake. Someone even asked me, "Do you think that you will get to Heaven by being a skeleton?"

By the time I was nineteen years old, I was fully involved in the ministry. I had many sheep who looked up to me for direction and prayer. By 1980 I was a strong preacher and leader of the Scripture Union fellowship. The point I am making is that ministry is possible alongside other pursuits.

I entered the university in October 1982. I was privileged to be a medical student - one of the most difficult and time-consuming courses. Whilst in the university I began a Christian fellowship, still in existence today.

During my fourth year, I began to establish the foundations for a church. I then became a pastor and was acknowledged as such whilst I was still a medical student.

During this time I was not being paid by anyone to do the work of the ministry. Neither did I slacken in my academic work. On the contrary, I did extremely well and won prizes in the medical school. I applied wisdom and sacrificed my leisure time so that I could be involved in ministry.

These are the two keys to being a shepherd – *sacrifice and wisdom.*

What is the main task of a pastor? Is it to perform funerals and officiate weddings? Certainly not! These are certainly duties of a minister but they are not the main duties. If your ministry has deteriorated to the point where your main functions are to conduct marriages and bury people, then you need to read your Bible again! The main duty of a minister is to fulfil the Great Commission.

**Go ye therefore, and teach all nations, baptizing them in the name of the Father, and of the Son, and of the Holy Ghost: Teaching them to observe all things whatsoever I have commanded you: and, lo, I am with you alway, even unto the end of the world. Amen.**

**Matthew 28:19, 20**

The reason why it is called the Great Commission is because it is the great commandment to all ministers. It is sad to see ministers of the Gospel who have become mere social functionaries. Sometimes pastors are under pressure to be accepted by society.

As a result, they want to do nice things that relate to health, education, etc., so that they may gain the approval of society.

Apostle Peter came under the same pressure to leave his principal duties and to perform mainly social tasks.

And in those days, when the number of the disciples was multiplied, there arose a murmuring of the Grecians against the Hebrews, because their widows were neglected in the daily ministration. Then the twelve called the multitude of the disciples unto them, and said, It is not reason that we should leave the word of God, and serve tables.

**Wherefore, brethren, look ye out among you seven men of honest report, full of the Holy Ghost and wisdom, whom we may appoint over this business. BUT WE WILL GIVE OURSELVES CONTINUALLY TO PRAYER, AND TO THE MINISTRY OF THE WORD.**

**Acts 6:1-4**

You can see from this Scripture that Peter's main duty was to pray and to minister the Word. This is something that can be done by shepherds. Shepherds can be taught to visit and counsel younger Christians. Shepherds can be taught how to preach. Shepherds can be taught how to witness. Shepherds can be taught how to minister the Word with power. Shepherds can be taught to make spiritual gains through prayer. What I have just described is the work of a pastor.

What is needed is a systematic approach of training shepherds to become full fledged ministers. Do not limit a shepherd because he is a professional in another field. **Do not say that your doctors, lawyers, architects, carpenters, engineers, tailors, masons, nurses and secretaries, cannot be pastors. They can!!** I recently visited one of our churches pastored by a female nurse. I realized that there were hundreds of people in the church and I gave glory to God.

In a large house there are many vessels. God is using all kinds of people. Do not limit God to what YOU think with your little experience and limited knowledge.

**But in a great house there are not only vessels of gold and of silver, but also of wood and of earth; and some to honour, and some to dishonour. If a man therefore purge himself from these, he shall be a vessel unto honour, sanctified, and meet for the master's use, and prepared unto every good work.**

**2 Timothy 2:20, 21**

When I was in my first year at the university, I was told by the Christian fellowship that *I could not be a leader because I was a medical student.* Medical students were considered too busy to be involved in ministry work. How unfortunate! They had effectively eliminated a whole group of potential leaders from the fellowship. This is what many pastors do. They look at the doctors in the church and think to themselves, *"Sit down quietly, receive your Sunday sermons and pay your tithes. Be a nice principled Christian doctor who does not perform abortions and you will please God!!"*

I want you to know that a doctor can also please God by winning souls. It is true that God wants principled doctors. But God also wants doctors who will win souls and do the work of ministry. Today, I have doctors who own clinics and at the same time pastor churches with hundreds of members. Today, I have many architects who do full-time architectural work and are very fruitful in ministry. I have pastors who work in banks and pastor large churches. **There are pastors who are teachers, pharmacists, university lecturers, accountants, students, doctors, nurses, army officers, civil servants, air conditioner repairers, computer scientists, computer technicians, businessmen, lawyers, and the list goes on!**

Some years ago, our church came under investigation by the tax office. The investigators could not believe that our long list of pastors were lay people who were not paid by the church.

If pastors gain the understanding that their members can do much more than just give money to the church, they would have helped themselves and their churches a great deal. That is what this book is about - showing how you can become a shepherd and be involved in the ministry.

Please do not misunderstand me; not every person who is active in ministry must become a full fledged minister. Some of the people will function as ordinary shepherds. But there are others who have the call of God upon their lives and will rise to be in full time ministry.

## The Pineapple Patch

One day as I was walking on a hillside I saw something which I want to share with you. I was praying in tongues and walking along a footpath on one of the hills in Ghana. The entire hillside was covered with wild bushes and tall untamed grass. As I walked along, I saw a section within the wild grass measuring about 20 meters by 20 meters. In that particular section there were neatly planted pineapple plants. I could see the baby pineapples sprouting. That section of the hillside was very different from the rest of the surroundings.

The Spirit of the Lord spoke to me and said, "That section of the hillside is different because certain seeds have been planted there. That area of the hillside is different because some special investment has been made on that patch of ground."

The Lord told me that the rest of the hillside can be likened to the general congregation which receives the general rainfall. The special patch of ground which was yielding pineapples can be likened to the leadership of the church. If you invest in a particular area, it will yield what you want it to yield.

**Many people do not invest in their leaders. If you invest in potential leaders, you will harvest a crop of well-seasoned leaders.** I spend more time with my leaders than I do with the general congregation.

The teachings in this book are examples of some of the things I have taught ordinary people over the years.

This investment has turned many people into shepherds! Invest specially in leaders and potential pastors and they will grow up to become great ministers!

I have heard people criticizing me for starting churches with people whom they consider not to be pastors. Come a little closer and learn what really happens in the church. For years, and at great expense, I have been holding Shepherds' Camps and training people to become shepherds of God's sheep. We constantly have pastoral training sessions for people who want to be in the ministry. *I am constantly encouraging my lay people to be more than principled citizens of the country.* I want them to be soul winners for Jesus. I want them to be shepherds of God's flock. I want them to fulfill the Great Commission.

Dear friend, I wrote this book for you! God told me to write it! God has a ministry for you. Please do not go to Heaven and discover that you did not even start your ministry before you died! Take what you are reading seriously and learn the art of shepherding and pastoring. Discover for yourself the joy of serving God as a shepherd!

## Chapter 5

# Sharing the Burden

**And the Lord said unto Moses, Gather unto me seventy men of the elders of Israel, whom thou knowest to be the elders of the people, and officers over them; and bring them unto the tabernacle of the congregation, that they may stand there with thee. And I will come down and talk with thee there: and I will take of the spirit which is upon thee, and will put it upon them; and they shall BEAR THE BURDEN of the people with thee, that thou bear it not thyself alone.**

**Numbers 11:16, 17**

One of the most difficult tasks in life is to lead people. The Bible teaches us that Moses delivered the Israelites from bondage, yet he had a difficult time handling them. The job that Moses did is the job that all pastors have to do.

God graciously gave Moses spectacular and sensational miracles. These signs and wonders helped to establish his authority over God's flock. In spite of this, the burden of leading the people was very heavy on Moses. The Bible calls it a burden – and that is what it is!

## People Have Problems

If you have a pastor's heart and love people, you cannot disassociate yourself from their problems. Their problems will become your problems and their burdens will affect you!

When God wants to use you to minister to a large number of people, he will expect you to share the burden of His divine call upon your life. Failure to share this burden will simply mean that you may collapse or come to a standstill in ministry. There are many standstill churches around. They grow to a point but can grow no further. The reason being they fail to share the burden of ministry.

A balanced church is one that has people of all sorts within it; young, the old, educated and uneducated, rich and poor, and male and female. Every pastor will fall into one of these categories. It must be your goal to incorporate all sections of the church to help in the development and growth of the ministry. In other words, all sorts must be drafted in, to the share the burden. You will find that the category of people, who you have written off, as far as ministry is concerned, would be able to contribute greatly to the ministry.

I notice that most churches exclude the educated and rich from involvement in ministry. Usually, the rich are only expected to contribute money to the church.

Similarly, the educated are just expected to improve the cosmetic image of the church. However, I have found both of these groups of people to be very productive and useful spiritually.

I have many medical doctors, specialists, lecturers, architects, and engineers, who are all serving as shepherds. These shepherds are sharing the burden of ministry alongside me.

**The burden of the ministry cannot be borne by one person.** It is simply impossible. From today, if you want to have a greater ministry than what you currently have, learn to share the burden.

Sometimes people do not share the burden because they want to take all of the glory for themselves. They want people to feel that they are the only ones with a supernatural gift. They want people to show appreciation to them alone. Others are afraid of rebellion in the camp. Many senior pastors fear their assistants will outshine them one day. Fear not, only believe! You cannot expand without trusting people. The work is so great that you will never ever be able to do it all alone. There is too much space in the sky for two birds to collide.

I want to show you seven reasons why it is such a burden to pastor people.

# Seven Reasons Why Pastoring People Is Such a Burden

**1. People are a burden because they are ungrateful and forgetful.**

> **...in the last days... men shall be... unthankful...**
> **2 Timothy 3:1, 2**

You can notice ungratefulness in people by the way they complain. Moses led the Israelites out of bondage and slavery and yet they murmured and complained bitterly against him. Aaron even had to make a golden calf to calm them down.

When something minute goes wrong, you may be surprised at the actions of people you have ministered to. Many easily forget what you have done for them. This is because the things a pastor does are often not physically tangible, but spiritual. Most tend to think that the pastor has done nothing for them. Others go a step further and commit evil towards you after you have been a blessing to them. Don't be shocked! The prophet Jeremiah experienced the same thing from his people. He said,

> **Shall evil be recompensed for good?**
> **Jeremiah 18:20a**

Once a pastor told a very disturbing story. He said that he was surprised when one of his church members came to his house one night to assault him. He couldn't believe that this young man whom he had led to Christ, trained up in the Lord, blessed his marriage and helped him through various crises would attack him in that manner.

Dear friend, do not be surprised! Do not expect gratitude from man; expect your rewards from God. Hezekiah was blessed. But he did not "render again". That means he did not show gratitude for all the blessings he had received.

> **But Hezekiah RENDERED NOT AGAIN according to the benefit done unto him...**
> **2 Chronicles 32:25**

This is the nature of man. This is the nature of the people God wants you to lead.

## 2. People are a burden because they will betray you.

Though Judas walked and ministered with Jesus for three years, he eventually betrayed him for a small amount of money. Betrayal is a part of ministry. It is also a part of life. If you have yet to experience betrayal, I can assure you that you will. The disturbing thing about betrayal is that it is done by people who are close to you.

You are not greater than your master Jesus! The fact that someone may one day betray you, makes it very difficult for you to happily interact and flow with him. Look closely at the ministry of any great man of God. You will discover that they have all had their fair share of traitors. All of this contributes to the burden and difficulty of ministry.

> **Yea, mine own familiar friend, in whom I trusted, which did eat of my bread, hath lifted up his heel against me.**
>
> **Psalm 41:9**

## 3. People are a burden because they are wicked.

Alexander, the coppersmith did Paul a lot of harm in his ministry.

> **Alexander the coppersmith did me much evil: the Lord reward him according to his works:**
>
> **2 Timothy 4:14**

I have experienced wickedness from people who have lifted themselves up to fight and oppose me. There are times when my ministry and very existence have become a source of work for such wicked individuals; their work being fighting, slandering and that of opposition. Without my existence, I think some people may not even have a job to do!

If you are not resolute in ministry, you could easily decide to leave these harassments behind and move on to a more peaceful existence in some secular job.

## 4. People are a burden because they can abandon you suddenly.

Paul experienced sudden desertions by some of his colleagues, like Demas. I remember one young man whom I trained. He was about to take up an important position in the ministry that we had been preparing for, for over a year. On the day he was to fill the position, he suddenly informed me that he was leaving the country. I couldn't believe my ears! All of our months of preparation meant nothing to him. He just abandoned ship without notice. These experiences are all part of the ministry. Abandonment also occurred under the ministry of Apostle Paul.

**For Demas hath forsaken me...**

**2 Timothy 4:10**

Because people can abandon you at any time, it is burdensome to lead them. But God wants us to help share the burden of His people. God wants us to be involved in His work. God wants us to be shepherds!

## 5. People are a burden because they are equalizers, disrespectful and impudent.

**And Miriam and Aaron spake against Moses... Hath the Lord indeed spoken only by Moses? HATH HE NOT SPOKEN ALSO BY US?**

**Numbers 12:1, 2**

Miriam and Aaron (the closest assistants and closest relatives) were now speaking against Moses. They most probably said things like, "God also speaks by us," and "Are you the only one?"

With time, familiarity creeps in and people now consider you as an equal. They tend to think, "We can all do it. What's the big deal? You are no different from us!"

This is unfortunate, but real. People easily take you for granted. They murmur and complain against you, forgetting all that you have done for them. When they lose their temper, you will find church members speaking to you like a little child.

## "You Remind Me of my Father"

One church member approached her pastor after Sunday service. The pastor thought she was about to compliment him for the powerful sermon he had just preached.

She started, "Pastor, you know something? I felt I should tell you that you remind me of my father."

"Oh really?" the pastor responded.

She continued, "He was so full of himself and so are you!"

The pastor was taken aback but he had to smile and continue as though he had received a compliment. The church member was telling the pastor exactly what she thought of him. This is why people are a burden.

> **Now Korah...and Dathan...and Abiram...and ...rose up before Moses...and said...WHEREFORE THEN LIFT YE UP YOURSELVES [Moses and Aaron] above the congregation of the Lord?**
>
> **Numbers 16:1-3**

These rebels apparently thought that Moses felt he was too "big for his own shoes".

### 6. People are a burden because they are disobedient and rebellious.

Samuel confronted Saul and asked him why he had not obeyed the Lord fully. One of the difficult things every pastor will have to come to terms with is that in spite of all the good things you preach, many people are still disobedient and continue to live in sin.

I used to be amazed at the extent of spiritual rebellion found in the Body of Christ. But that is human nature.

**Wherefore then didst thou not obey the voice of the Lord, but didst fly upon the spoil, and didst evil in the sight of the Lord?**

**1 Samuel 15:19**

7.  **People are a burden because they do not understand and do not respond.**

**When any one heareth the word of the kingdom, and UNDERSTANDETH IT NOT...**

**Matthew 13:19**

Sometimes people do not understand the Word. Often they do not understand why you have to do fundraising. Many times, I have to explain that people are giving to build a nice church where *they* can have *their* weddings, baby dedications and other ceremonies. Leading people who have all the above characteristics: ungratefulness, disloyalty, etc., is a major task.

One person cannot do it alone. The burden must be shared with others. Sharing the burden is hard work. The people will be angry with you for trying to help them. People need help but when you try to give it to them, they attack you.

## Distributing the Burden

The principal strategy for distributing the burden is to involve men and women in ministry. No church is capable of employing an endless number of people. Every church has a limit to its resources.

It is not possible to pay salaries and rent an unlimited number of houses for the staff of the ministry. Full-time staff are limited in the amount of work that they can do. In my ministry, I oversee more than one thousand five hundred churches and several thousand people. We have over one thousand pastors and trainee pastors within the ministry.

# Stop Pretending...

A pastor is neither a banker nor an accountant. He is a shepherd. Shepherds must be in the fields moving amongst the sheep and ministering to them.

Let the pastors do pastoral work, and let the secular people do their work. Shepherds can join the pastors to share the burden of the people. Let your shepherds know that they are called to share the burden of ministry with you. They will share the burden on earth and they will share the burden of accounting for the sheep in heaven. What is the burden on earth? It is the burden of praying, visiting, counselling and interacting with the sheep. What is the burden in heaven? It is the burden of answering for each and every soul that God gave to you.

The burden of leading sheep cannot be borne by one person or just a few people who supposedly have a "call". The burden of accounting for hundreds of different people cannot be borne by one person. When I stand before the judgement seat and God asks me about some souls in Canada, I intend to mention the name of the pastor there and ask the Lord to inquire from him. When the Lord asks me about some souls in Navrongo, in the north of Ghana, I will immediately tell the Lord, "Please ask my dear pastor who is in charge of that branch." It is impossible for one person to answer for such a large burden of souls.

> **...for they watch for your souls, AS THEY THAT MUST GIVE ACCOUNT, that they may do it with joy...**
>
> **Hebrews 13:17**

Every pastor will have a lot to answer for when he stands before the Lord in heaven. Your burden is to lead all your sheep to heaven. Make sure you lose none of them. Every true pastor's motto should be, "Of all that you have given me, I have lost none!" (John 6:39, John 17:12; and John 18:9)

Moses was breaking down under the burden of leading the entire flock. God saw this and decided to take of the "spirit" that was on Moses and put it on the seventy leaders "to bear the burden" with him.

**And the Lord said unto Moses, Gather unto me SEVENTY MEN of the elders of Israel... THAT THEY MAY STAND [work] THERE WITH THEE.**
**Numbers 11:16**

Involving students, workers, and professionals help to distribute the burden to all saints in the church.

The Lord wants us to be fruitful no matter what we do in this life. In the universities, I have established churches and have entrusted the preaching and pastoring responsibilities to a few students. I am very proud of these student ministers because of the great job that they have done on their respective campuses. I don't have to rush to the university every Sunday morning to minister the Word. Ordinary saints should please join in and work together.

The saints must be perfected (prepared, trained) to do the work of the ministry. Ordinary saints can do the work. Laymen can also work for God.

**For the perfecting of the saints, for the work of the ministry, for the edifying of the body of Christ:**
**Ephesians 4:12**

## Chapter 6

# Take up the Spiritual Burden

The spiritual burden is a different type of burden but it is an important one. God will only use you if you have a burden. If there is no burden, God will not use you. For example, if you want to heal the sick and cast out devils you need to have a genuine burden to have miracles of healing.

I had a burden to preach and to teach. Preaching and teaching bring deliverance. Preaching and teaching are powerful. I emphasize the Word of God whilst others emphasize other things. You cannot emphasize the Word of God unless you believe it is a powerful tool of deliverance.

Compassion is a key starting point for all ministries.

## Jesus Had a Burden

Jesus was moved with compassion when he saw the sheep without a shepherd.

> **But when he saw the multitudes, HE WAS MOVED WITH COMPASSION ON THEM, because they fainted, and were scattered abroad, as sheep having no shepherd.**
>
> **Matthew 9:36**

Jesus was moved with compassion when he saw the multitudes.

> **And Jesus, when he came out, saw much people, AND WAS MOVED WITH COMPASSION TOWARD THEM...**
>
> **Mark 6:34**

No one can minister effectively without a genuine burden. Jesus' burden was to keep all that the Father had given him. The reason I know this was a burden on him was that he kept on repeating this particular statement.

> ...of all which he hath given me I should lose nothing...
>
> **John 6:39**

> ...those that thou gavest me I have kept, and none of them is lost, but the son of perdition...
>
> **John 17:12**

> That the saying might be fulfilled, which he spake, Of them which thou gavest me have I lost none.
>
> **John 18:9**

People who don't have a burden for souls, are often motivated by money, fame, power or some other ulterior motive.

## Paul Had a Burden

Paul's desire (burden) for Israel was that they might be saved.

> **Brethren, my heart's DESIRE and prayer to God for Israel is, that they might be saved.**
>
> **Romans 10:1**

Paul had great heaviness and sorrow in his heart for his people.

> **I say the truth in Christ, I lie not, my conscience also bearing me witness in the Holy Ghost, That I have GREAT HEAVINESS and CONTINUAL SORROW in my heart.**
>
> **Romans 9:1-2**

## How to Develop a Genuine Shepherdorial Burden

If you are the senior pastor, you can sensitize people towards the burden of ministry. The shepherdorial burden is the burden of not losing any of the sheep that God has given you.

This burden drives a pastor to look for the lost, pray for the sheep, and to visit them. It is that burden that leads us to fast and pray so that the sheep will not fall away.

The pastor's heart and attitude is that he doesn't want to lose any of the people he has in his ministry or church. It is that attitude that makes the pastor leave the ninety-nine people to follow the one lost sheep.

It should be that the only people who leave your church are "sons of perdition". Sometimes people who leave are not "sons of perdition" but genuine people who we didn't care for. People who didn't receive the shepherd's attention!

## 1. Do not be overcome by your own problems and burdens

When you get to the point where your own problems and burdens do not weigh you down, then you have taken the first step towards having a genuine shepherdorial burden. As long as the burden for your own problems weigh you down, you will not be able to think about God's work. Genuine ministry begins when you can separate yourself from your own burdens and take on the burdens of others.

I always remember the example of Kathryn Khulman, an American healing evangelist. She had a strong burden for the sick to be healed. However, she herself was said to be very ill with a serious heart condition whilst she ministered to the sick. She did not think of her own problems as she ministered to the needs of others.

## 2. Praying for a burden

You can pray to God for a burden for His work. I remember a retreat I attended in 1982, just before I went to university. It was held at the Legon Botanical Gardens. It was a seven-hour prayer meeting from 10:00 a.m. to 5:00 p.m. What a memorable event!

Guess what we prayed for? We prayed for a burden. We didn't ask God to bless our ministries, we asked Him to give us a genuine burden for His work. I believe that is why God has given me a burden for His work, because I asked for it. I spent seven hours praying for a burden!

*Dive into the work and the burden will come.*

You cannot do the ministry work for long without realizing the great need of mankind for the Word and power of God. As you do God's will, a burden for the harvest will come upon you.

*Chapter 7*

# Poimen

## Who Was Jesus Christ?

...I am the bread of life...

John 6:35

...I am from above...

John 8:23

...Before Abraham was, I am.

John 8:58

...I am the light of the world.

John 9:5

I am the door...

John 10:9

I am the good shepherd...

John 10:11

...I am the Son of God?

John 10:36

...I am the resurrection, and the life...

John 11:25

Ye call me Master and Lord: and ye say well; for so I am.

John 13:13

...I am the way, the truth, and the life...

John 14:6

I am the vine...

John 15:5

...Thou sayest that I am a king.  To this end was I born...

John 18:37

I am Alpha and Omega, the beginning and the ending...

Revelation 1:8

...I am the first and the last...

Revelation 1:17

J esus Christ was many things to us.  He called himself different things at different times.  At one time he said he was the way, the truth and the life.  He announced that he was the door.  He declared that he was the bread of life and the light of the world.

But one of the most important things that Jesus proclaimed was that he was the good shepherd.

I am the good shepherd...

John 10:11

# What Is Poimen?

What did Jesus mean when he said he was a good shepherd? The word shepherd in John 10:11 is translated from the Greek word *poimen* (pronounced "*poy-mane*").

It is this same word, poimen, which is translated pastor in Ephesians 4:11.

And he gave some, apostles; and some, prophets; and some, evangelists; and some, pastors [poimen] and teachers;

Ephesians 4:11

The word 'shepherd' is interchangeable with the word 'pastor'.  So what the Lord was really saying was, "I am the good pastor".  Throughout the Bible, Jesus referred to himself as a shepherd or a pastor.  Jesus Christ is the perfect example of a good pastor.

The pastoral office is very important because without it many things cannot work. Remember that the sheep were scattered and lost, not because they didn't have an apostle or prophet, but because they didn't have a pastor.

**But when he saw the multitudes, he was moved with compassion on them, because they fainted, and were scattered abroad, as sheep having no shepherd [pastor].**

**Matthew 9:36**

I am not saying that prophets and apostles are not important. They are! But without a good pastor there will be no gathering of God's people.

The Bible says that sheep without shepherds fainted. This means they were distressed and harassed.

## I'm Having a Heart Attack... Somebody Call a Dentist!

In the medical arena there are ophthalmologists (eye doctors), cardiothoracic surgeons (heart doctors), and dentists (teeth doctors). If you ever had a heart problem, you would certainly not want a dentist to operate on your heart! Neither would I! Dentists are specialists for the teeth and not for the heart.

In the secular world, people have grown to respect these different specialties and have allowed them to function well within their own field. Specialists increase the individual's safety and allow for the special needs of everyone to be met.

We must learn to accord similar specialties to Christian ministers. Today, everyone in the ministry is called "pastor". However, many of those who claim to be pastors are no more a pastor than I am the Heavyweight Boxing Champion of the world!

In the Old Testament, anyone who intruded into a holy place or office, in which they had not been called, were struck dead by a Holy God who does not accept such intrusions.

In my few years of ministry, I have noticed many people without the shepherding gift standing in the office of pastor. Consequently, some of these people either have failed in ministry or are experiencing a gradual disintegration of their ministries. This is not because they are evil, but simply because *a dentist cannot operate on a heart.* God gives different gifts to everyone. It is time for us to discover our gifts and stay with our special callings.

One of the key roles of a shepherd is to lead sheep.

> **The Lord is my shepherd; I shall not want. He maketh me to lie down in green pastures: HE LEADETH ME...**
>
> **Psalm 23:1, 2**

# What Is the Gift of Government?

In 1 Corinthians 12:28, the Bible talks about the gifts of governments. The word "government" is translated from the Greek word, kubernesis, which means a steering, pilotage, or guiding. I believe that this gift of governments is the same thing as the office of a shepherd or pastor.

Essentially the gift of government is used to lead and guide people. The shepherd is to use this gifting to guide the sheep to "good places" (green pastures). This gift of governments is a special gift from God and is therefore not to be enterprised nor taken in hand wantonly or unadvisedly by anybody.

We need to soberly reflect on the implications of leading people. When someone does not have the ability to govern in the natural world, the whole nation can be thrown into chaos.

There are bad governments everywhere. This is obvious by the state of poverty, war, and instability that exist in such countries. That is the reason why there is so much fuss about who is elected into the seat of government. The government means so much to everyone. It may mean the difference between death and life, poverty and prosperity.

That is why there is so much commotion over which government will come into power. There must be equal concern in the church about who is allowed to become a pastor. With poor government, and incapable people at the helm of affairs in the church, we are headed for anarchy and chaos.

God's Word must be our guiding post. Things not based on the Word of God have a limited life span. In the beginning, they may look flashy and appealing, but with time, they will crumble!

It is time for evangelists to leave the church and go out where the sinners are.

# Who Should Govern, Prophet or Pastor?

You will notice certain peculiar things when an evangelist or prophet is in charge of a church. On your first visit, the charisma and the inspiration of the leader may impress you.

Apostles, prophets and evangelists are very inspirational and impressive speakers. But remember, a church is not governed on impressive speeches and powerful prophecies.

*A church is not sustained by miracles.* A local church is to be run by a pastor—a good shepherd (poimen). Someone with the ability to govern a local body of people. Somebody with the ability to lead people successfully to a good place (green pastures). Someone with the gift of governments (1 Corinthians 12:28).

# They Don't Know That They Don't Know!

As you continue attending a church that is pastored by an evangelist, you will probably notice some amount of disorganization and mismanagement. **People who are not pastors, struggle with the day-to-day administration of their churches.**

Often these out-of-place ministers are accused of evil deeds. Knowing some of them personally, I realize that they have no evil intentions. It is just that they simply do not have the gift of governments (administration, management). The sad thing is that sometimes they don't even know that they don't have the ability.

## The Broken Amplifier

I remember once visiting a church headed by someone, obviously called to be an evangelist. After I finished ministering, I heard the minister chide the whole church about an amplifier and other equipment that had not been repaired.

The question I asked myself was this, "What does the repairing of equipment have to do with the whole congregation?" The maintenance of the equipment should have nothing to do with the congregation, but rather with the administration of the church. A church must be able to run its affairs properly.

This man of God spoke to the congregation about money matters and other intricate details that had nothing to do with the general crowd. They were matters of internal management. At a point, tears came to my eyes as I watched this evangelist, helplessly and hopelessly struggle to govern the local body.

The evangelist's rightful place was out on the harvest fields, bringing multitudes to Christ, performing miracles, signs and wonders (not governing a local assembly). As soon as such a person sits in the seat of government, he becomes an oddity. In fact, you can become a byword and a laughing stock after a while!

## The Evangelist Was Feeding Them "Junk Food"

Churches not run by *called* pastors are sustained by waves of inspirational meetings. The sheep are not systematically taught Bible principles and doctrines. Rather, they are fed on a diet of inspirational, highly motivating and emotional meals every week.

No Christian can survive on eating "junk food" everyday; they need a well-balanced diet!

These churches are full of babies who are not interested in the Bible. Therefore, there is no stability in the membership. They have what I call a *floating crowd*. Every week you will see an entirely different group of people attending their services. In order to grow, people need a regular diet of the Word of God.

> **And Jesus [the Word] said unto them, I am the bread of life: he that cometh to me shall never hunger; and he that believeth on me shall never thirst.**
>
> **John 6:35**

Motivation is different from feeding. There are churches that are full of highly motivated but empty shells.

What am I trying to say? It is time for us to allow the church to be governed by individuals with the gift of governments. It is time for shepherds to take their rightful place at the helm of the local church. It is time for people to be able to say like the Lord Jesus – I am a good shepherd or pastor.

## Chapter 8

# Different Levels of the Anointing

**O**ne thing that we must be aware of is that there are different levels of anointing within the same office or calling. Though a group of people may be called to minister as prophets, they will operate in this ministerial office with varying levels of anointing. I want to show you this truth from three different points in Scripture.

### 1. Two levels of the prophetic anointing

Notice the example of the prophets Elijah and Elisha. Though they both operated in the office of a prophet, Elisha eventually operated on a level of anointing that was twice that of Elijah's. The Bible records that Elisha asked to be able to operate on a level two times higher than that of Elijah, his father-in-ministry.

> **...Elijah said unto Elisha, Ask what I shall do for thee, before I be taken away from thee. And Elisha said, I pray thee, LET A DOUBLE PORTION OF THY SPIRIT BE UPON ME.**
>
> **2 Kings 2:9**

Obviously, Elisha knew that there was something higher within the office of the prophet that he could attain. He did not want to be something else, like a pastor or teacher. He wanted to remain a prophet, but within that office, he wanted to be a prophet of a higher degree. This principle applies to the pastoral office.

You too can desire to go higher within any calling that God has set you in! Ask and you shall receive! Elisha asked and he got what he asked for. Jesus said, **"If ye abide in me, and my words abide in you, ye shall ask what ye will, and it shall be done unto you"** (John 15:7).

## 2.   The highest level of anointing

Jesus ministered as a pastor. He was someone who operated in a limitless measure of the anointing. In other words, Jesus operated at the highest possible level within the gifting of a pastor.

> **For he whom God hath sent speaketh the words of God: FOR GOD GIVETH NOT THE SPIRIT BY MEASURE UNTO HIM.**
>
> **John 3:34**

## 3.   You can notice different levels

Apostle Paul asked the Corinthians to notice certain things about their calling.

> **FOR YE SEE YOUR CALLING, brethren, how that not many wise men after the flesh, not many mighty, not many noble, are called:**
>
> **1 Corinthians 1:26**

As you observe different people in the office of a shepherd, **it is obvious that some are operating in a higher shepherding anointing.** Just observe different ministers operating in the same office. You will soon notice that some speak with much more power than others do.

There are times that I have sat in meetings and heard great men of God preaching from the same verses that I have preached. I then ask myself, "Why is the effect so different when this man preaches from the same simple scripture?" The answer is - different levels of anointing. Yes, that minister was ministering the same thing, but with a different level of power and anointing.

You will discover that larger crowds gather to hear someone who is on a higher level of anointing. One of the characteristics of the anointing is that it attracts crowds.

**Pastors who are operating on a higher level of pastoral anointing tend to have larger churches than shepherds**

**who have less of the pastoral gift.** In reality, some shepherds can have only three church members whilst others have three thousand.

This does not mean that the shepherd with three members is not a shepherd. Just that he is a shepherd with a different level of anointing.

You will notice that more miracles and revelations occur in a prophet who moves in a higher level of anointing. Elijah performed sixteen miracles, but Elisha had thirty-two spectacular miracles and revelations.

One of the ways we are expected to develop our calling and office is by observing what God is doing with you. You can actually see certain things about your calling and your office by watching yourself and observing your natural gifts. When I say natural gifts, I don't mean human talents. I mean God-given abilities for the ministry.

> **FOR YE SEE YOUR CALLING, brethren, how that not many wise men after the flesh, not many mighty, not many noble, are called:**
>
> **1 Corinthians 1:26**

## You Can See Your Calling

You can actually see things about your calling. There are two ways God puts you into an office. Sometimes God can actually tell you that from this time onwards He has called you and put you in an office. You are then expected to flow in that area and follow Him as He leads you step-by-step.

At other times, God expects you to notice your calling by seeing what you do naturally.

**Anytime you find yourself doing something effortlessly on a consistent basis, you may have a calling in that area.** You see (observe and notice things about) your calling (1 Corinthians 1:26).

## Chapter 9

# Fifteen Essential Features of Potential Shepherds

1.  **A personal relationship with God**

    **Draw nigh to God, and he will draw nigh to you. Cleanse your hands, ye sinners; and purify your hearts, ye double minded.**

    **James 4:8**

    Without a personal relationship with God, you are going nowhere and you cannot be a shepherd. A disciplined person who has consistent prayer and personal Bible study shows a deep relationship with God. Your reading and study of ministry related books compliments Bible study and is a good sign.

2.  **The interest in listening to preaching tapes and watching Word videos**

    **And the spirit entered into me when he spake unto me, and set me upon my feet, that I heard him that spake unto me.**

    **Ezekiel 2:2**

    People become spiritual when they listen to preaching messages. The Spirit enters into them. This is indicative of a person's personal interests and desires. The Bible says a pastor should not be greedy for money. Are they greedy for money or greedy for the Word?

3.  **The personal fasting life of the shepherd**

    **In weariness and painfulness, in watchings often, in hunger and thirst, in fastings often, in cold and nakedness.**

    **2 Corinthians 11:27**

This also shows commitment and preparedness to sacrifice. Someone who never fasts must be marked. If you cannot lay down your stomach, what else can you lay down?

## 4.   Availability for the work

**Wherefore of these men which have companied with us all the time that the Lord Jesus went in and out among us**

**Acts 1:21**

*Availability is the most important feature to look out for in a potential shepherd.* When the twelve apostles were looking for a replacement for Judas, they looked for somebody who had been around and available for the three years that Jesus had been in town. Availability is key to learning all you need to know about ministry. The major sacrifice of a shepherd is to make himself available in spite of his business and work schedule. Some people do not make the sacrifice to spend their evenings or Sundays doing extra work for the Lord. Many shepherds *work the whole day Sunday and many evenings throughout the week.* This is a big sacrifice. Someone who is not prepared to be available cannot do this job!

## 5.   The individual's financial input to the church

**Then one of the twelve, called Judas Iscariot, went unto the chief priests, and said unto them, what will ye give me, and I will deliver him unto you? And they covenanted with him for thirty pieces of silver.**

**And from that time he sought opportunity to betray him**

**Matthew 26:14-16**

Someone who is not committed financially is not committed at all. The Bible teaches us that if a person is not faithful with unrighteous mammon then he cannot be faithful with God's riches. Pastors who do not pay tithes and offerings should be dismissed—they are traitors in the making. Acquire and maintain a system of monitoring the tithes and offerings of all leaders in the church. You have a right to demand that those who claim to be shepherds be committed financially!

## 6. People handling skills

**A bishop then must be blameless, the husband of one wife, vigilant, sober, of good behaviour, given to hospitality, APT TO TEACH; not given to wine, NO STRIKER, not greedy of filthy lucre; but patient, not a brawler, not covetous**

**1 Timothy 3:2-3**

When the Bible says "apt to teach", it includes the ability to lead and influence by your personal lifestyle. Teaching includes being able to handle people of all sorts. A person who is quarrelsome is disqualified from being a pastor. "No striker" in 1 Timothy 3:3 means you are not to be *quarrelsome or cantankerous.*

## 7. Preaching and teaching skills

**And the things that thou hast heard of me among many witnesses, THE SAME commit thou to faithful men...**

**2 Timothy 2:2**

People who want to be shepherds must develop the ability to teach and to preach. The principal duty of a shepherd is to feed the flocks. Someone who wants to be a pastor must demonstrate experience in preaching and teaching. The best way to learn how to preach is listen to preaching tapes and preach the same thing. Timothy was told to preach the same thing that he had heard Paul preaching.

## 8. An interest in evangelism

**How think ye? if a man have an hundred sheep, and one of them be gone astray, doth he not leave the ninety and nine, and goeth into the mountains, and seeketh that which is gone astray?**

**Matthew 18:12**

Assess the interest of the potential shepherd in winning souls. Soul winning is the ultimate job for the whole church. Jesus was a good pastor. He said, "I am the good shepherd" (John 10:14). But he also said, "I came to seek and save that which was lost." (Luke 19:10). *Therefore, a good shepherd seeks to save sinners, which are lost.*

If you are not interested in souls I question whether you have a genuine call to be a shepherd.

## 9. Visiting, counselling and organizational abilities

**And the servant of the Lord must not strive; but be gentle unto all men, apt to teach, patient**
**2 Timothy 2:22**

These are the three most used skills by shepherds. These fall under the qualification—apt to teach. A person who does not love people enough to visit them is not a pastor at heart. Shepherds must be able to organize people together in order to be able to teach them the Word. Counselling is the art of giving the counsel of the Word of God to people.

## 10. Having a stable and happy marriage

**For if a man know not how to rule his own house, how shall he take care of the church of God?**
**1 Timothy 3:5**

A person with a stormy and unhappy marriage is not likely to be a good shepherd. The Bible says in 1 Timothy 3:5, "For if a man know not how to rule his own house, how shall he take care of the church of God?" I have learnt from experience that many of the problems pastors have to solve are related to marriage. If the pastor himself is unable to gain control of his own marriage, what will he say to others? He will be forced to be a hypocrite and a liar, giving advice about things he himself does not practice. Ezra 7:10 gives a very important principle, it says, "Ezra had prepared his heart to seek the law of the Lord, and to do it, and to teach…" It is very important to do things before you teach them!

## 11. Catching the spirit of the leader

And Moses went out, and told the people the words of the Lord, and gathered the seventy men of the elders of the people, and set them round about the tabernacle.

**And the Lord came down in a cloud, and spake unto him, and TOOK OF THE SPIRIT THAT WAS UPON HIM, AND GAVE IT UNTO THE SEVENTY ELDERS: and it came to pass, that, when the spirit rested upon them, they prophesied, and did not cease**

**Numbers 11:24-25**

Choose someone who has caught the spirit of the leader. Shepherds and other pastors must operate in the same spirit or anointing of the senior pastor or founder of the church. This is the principle that God first set into motion in the days of Moses and his seventy elders. In Numbers 11 God took the same anointing that was on Moses and put it on seventy elders. From that time they all operated in the same spirit. This is important if you want to have a very large network of churches. It helps prevent disunity and disintegration of the Body into different factions with various opinions.

## 12. Your relationship with the opposite sex

**Rebuke not an elder, but INTREAT him as a father; and the younger men as brethren; the elder women as mothers; THE YOUNGER AS SISTERS, WITH ALL PURITY**

**1 Timothy 5:1-2**

Watch the relationship that potential shepherds have with the opposite sex. I encourage people to marry and to marry early - this brings stability. It also helps to prevent unwholesome relationships with the opposite sex.

## 13. Loyalty

**Deacons likewise must be men of dignity, NOT DOUBLE-TONGUED, or addicted to much wine or fond of sordid gain,**

**1 Timothy 3:8**

A deacon must not be double tongued according to 1 Timothy 3:8. The word double-tongued comes from the Greek word dilogos. It means liars, people who say different things to different people about the same subject. This person has two tongues. One is full of praise and good reports to the senior pastor. The other is full of traitorous, sarcastic, and disloyal comments when the pastor is not around.

Another interesting revelation is when the Bible says wives of deacons should not be slanderous. **The Greek word for slanderer is diabolos, which means devils.** If you have pastors' wives or pastors who are slanderous, it means your church is full of devils. If your church is full of devils how will it grow? How will it improve when you literally have human devils occupying positions of influence and leadership? Pastoral positions must be occupied by people who are 100 percent loyal to the cause!

## 14. Having personal financial and job stability

**A double minded man is unstable in all his ways.**

**James 1:8**

People who are unstable in one area of their life are likely to be unstable in other areas. A person who keeps changing jobs may end up changing churches, wives and friends.

The Bible says that a double-minded man is unstable in ALL (not some) his ways.

## 15. A person with a vision

**WHERE THERE IS NO VISION, THE PEOPLE PERISH: but he that keepeth the law, happy is he.**

**Proverbs 29:18**

Some shepherds often struggle with the problem of dual vision. They have a vision to fulfil their secular aspirations on the one hand and to fulfil their call to ministry on the other. Sometimes pressure from secular work stamps out the fire of ministry in shepherds.

Shepherds must desire to go forward in the ministry in real and measurable terms. People generally think that you make **your vision. But I've come to learn that it is your vision that makes you what you are!**

## Chapter 10

# The Ministry: Work or Rest?

I remember when I first started out in full-time ministry. People would often ask my wife at work, "Where is your husband? Is he at home?"

One lady, a lawyer friend of hers once said, "Oh, so your husband doesn't work anymore!"

My wife would answer, "You have no idea how hard he works."

They thought that because I was no longer practicing medicine, I was no longer working. Many people think that all that the pastor does is to prepare one sermon a week and then deliver it on Sunday morning. Afterwards, he is free to sleep until the next Sunday.

Many times people have called either late in the morning or in the afternoon and have said, "Hullo, how are you pastor? Sorry to disturb your sleep."

I would think, "This man thinks I sleep all day and all night as well."

Then I would politely answer, "I was not sleeping."

I have never bothered to explain what I was doing. "It is a waste of time." I thought to myself. These and other remarks have made me realize that some people think that the ministry is one long restful occupation—an easier alternative to real and difficult jobs. From both the Bible and my experience, I have seen that there is no work like ministry work.

## Ministry Is Work!

**And he gave some, apostles; and some, prophets; and some, evangelists; and some, pastors and teachers;**

**For the perfecting of the saints, FOR THE WORK OF THE MINISTRY, for the edifying of the body of Christ:**

**Ephesians 4:11-12**

This interpretation is a bit clearer in the New International Version:

**...to prepare God's people for works of service...**

**Ephesians 4:12 (NIV)**

The saints are to be perfected for the work. This means that pastors are to perfect the saints so that they can join in the hard work of ministry. There was a man called Epaphras, a servant of Christ "always labouring fervently for you in prayers". This man was labouring, he wasn't resting.

Throughout the Bible, ministry has been described as work. When Jesus saw the multitudes who were fainting because of lack of a shepherd, He said, "The harvest is plenty but the labourers are few."

The Greek word translated labourer is the word ergates, which means a toiler, teacher, laborer and a worker.

**The ministry is toil and sweat.** I have found that out practically. Anybody who wants to be a shepherd must realize that he is not embarking on a game but real work. He will soon realize that being a pastor is not in title alone, but is real toil and labour. If ministry is work, what does it involve? What type of work is ministry work?

# Four Main Aspects of a Lay Minister's Work

I have a simple code that will help every pastor and shepherd to remember what work he or she is supposed to do. I have simply titled it P - V - C - I.

P for PRAYER

V for VISITATION

C for COUNSELLING

I for INTERACTION

## 1. Prayer

Prayer is the cardinal sustaining force of the church. I believe in praying for hours for the church. **There is a correlation between the amount of prayer put into the church by the eldership of the church and the growth of the church.**

In Korea, it is well known that the pastors pray for long hours. It is no surprise then that the largest churches in the world are found in that nation. It is the will of God to have large churches because there are many people who need to be saved.

I believe that every full-time pastor should try to pray for at least three hours every day. **Shepherds should pray for at least one or two hours a day.** I believe in long times of prayer. Shepherds should make it a point to get away from their busy schedules and wait on God for even longer periods. Jesus himself retreated to the wilderness and mountains to pray. Praying for whole days on retreats is a very important aspect of the shepherd's schedule.

The ministry is spiritual from beginning to end. There is a difference between a pastor and an administrator. The fact that you are doing accounting work in the church office does not mean that you are in full-time ministry.

Full-time ministry is full-time prayer and ministry of the Word.

> **...It is not reason that we should leave the word of God, and serve tables...But we will give ourselves continually to prayer, and to the ministry of the word.**
> **Acts 6:2-4**

Peter made it clear that his work was not arranging tables nor organizing food for his church members. His duty was to pray and minister the Word. In this code PVCI, the ministry of the word comes under counseling.

## 2.   Visitation

In Jeremiah 23:2, God makes it clear that one of the principal duties of pastors is to visit.

**Therefore thus saith the Lord God of Israel against the pastors…Ye have scattered my flock..and have not VISITED them…**

**Jeremiah 23:2**

It is quite clear from this, that shepherds are expected to visit their sheep in their homes. This is different from counselling in the office. It is also different from preaching and teaching from the pulpit. It is a special ministry. The greatest visitor on this earth was Jesus Christ. Since his visit, the world has never been the same again.

In my ministry, I have observed a difference between those members I have visited and those who have never been visited. Members who I have been able to visit have become very stable and hardly ever left the church.

## 3.   Counselling

Counselling involves ministering the counsels of God to people. You can do this through teaching a congregation or an individual.

Churches based on solid Bible teachings tend to grow. As the years go by, these churches grow larger and larger. It is like a flock that has been exposed to fields upon fields of green grass. The natural response is that the flock will be healthy, multiply and grow.

**You will find greater growth in churches which have strong teaching and preaching than in churches which emphasize miracles.**

I believe in miracles but I also believe in the ministration of the Word. Sheep don't feed on miracles, they feed on the Word.

## 4.  Interaction

A shepherd is supposed to interact with his sheep.  How can he interact properly if he is detached and aloof?  Pastors and shepherds must do what I call *"Deep Sea Fishing"*.

Deep Sea Fishing

What is the deep sea?  The deep sea is the mass of church members who stream in and out of church every Sunday morning. Many people attend our churches and nobody knows them or even talks with them.  Some come in and out for a while and then drop out.

It is the duty of shepherds and pastors to plunge into what I call the deep sea and conduct *Deep Sea Fishing*.  They are to move into the crowd of unknown faces and interact with them. They must befriend unknown people, talk with them, find out where they live, and establish a line of friendship.

# Everybody Wants to Feel Important!

Everybody wants to be known and to feel important.  Without this, they would move to a place where they can be known and feel important.  **All human beings have a psychological need to be identified and recognized!**

**It is that need that we try to meet by doing "deep sea fishing".**  How many people can the senior pastor talk to on a Sunday?  Not many!  But if several other shepherds join him to lovingly interact, a lot more of the work will be done!

After interacting, the pastors will get to know the people who do not belong to small groups within the church, but still need pastoral visits and care.  **"Deep sea fishing" will lead to you knowing many of your members and to establishing floating visitors in the church.**  All shepherds and pastors are expected to do a certain amount of *deep sea fishing* every Sunday.  That is why it is important for shepherds to be in church on Sunday and involve themselves in this all-important interaction – *deep sea fishing*.  It is not only the senior pastor that is preaching who has work to do. All other ranks of shepherds have a lot to do – *deep sea fishing.*

Why should a pastor be ushered away from his congregation as though he were a Head of State. Why should I be ushered quickly into my car when I finish ministering? Am I a Head of-state or a pastor?

I love to linger on in the church for hours after the service, interacting with different people.

I am not a Prime Minister. I am a pastor. Pastors are not chief executives; they are shepherds who are supposed to mingle with their sheep. The Bible says that the sheep know the voice of the good shepherd. How can they know your voice if they don't even see you?

# Five Characteristics of Ministry Work

No shepherd can claim to have joined the ranks of ministry workers until his activities have gotten certain characteristics. They are what I call the *Characteristics of Ministry Work.*

An activity moves out of the realm of playing, joking and pleasure and into the realm of work when it has the following characteristics. If you are involved in ministry and your activity does not have these characteristics, you may be doing something related to the ministry but it has not yet become "work".

## 1. Ministry work has "working hours".

Every true job has its own working hours. The work of the ministry has its own peculiar working hours. This often confuses people. They think pastors must be in the office from 9:00 a.m. to 5:00 p.m. like everybody else. Those are the hours of most secular offices. But we are not bankers nor accountants, we are pastors. No more banking hours for pastors! Nobody asks pilots to work from 9:00 a.m. to 5:00 p.m. Everybody knows that their working hours are peculiar and everyone accepts that reality.

I rarely ever go to the office at 8 o'clock in the morning. Most of my work is in the evenings, that is when the sheep have come from their workplaces and are available. That is when I can interact with, pray for and minister to them. Anyone who wants to be a shepherd must fix some working hours. These working hours should be your weekends (especially Sundays) and some evenings.

Someone may say, "Then it means I won't have anytime to rest at weekends." Well, that is the reality of being a shepherd. It means a little extra sacrifice for the kingdom. You may not be prepared to do the greater sacrifice of leaving your job, so you have to give up some of your leisure and resting times.

Sometimes, pastors go to work at 6:00 a.m. on Sunday mornings and leave at midnight. Sunday is the busiest and most important day for a pastor. It should be the case for every church. Many people do not realize that the time when sheep will be available is the time when the shepherds must be at work.

Pastors must counsel, visit, and teach Bible school classes throughout Sundays. Different services, meetings and activities must continue until evening. Someone may ask, "When do you rest?" Pastors rest on Mondays.

## 2. Ministry work consumes a large amount of time.

When an activity consumes just a few minutes of your time in a week, it cannot be called your "work". For instance, I drive my car for a few minutes every day but my work is not "driving" per se. It is something that I do *on my way to work*.

However, if driving a car, for example a taxi, were to become my work, I would not spend less than eight hours a day driving. Then, to me, driving would have become work!

**You cannot claim to be doing the "work" of the ministry until it actually consumes a reasonable amount of time in your week.** Give your weekends and evenings to God.

### 3.  Ministry work expends energy and money.

Everyone must realize that doing the work of the ministry involves spending a lot of energy. Do not be surprised if you get tired doing the work of a shepherd. It is only a sign that the activity has entered the realm of 'work'. You have now begun to do the work of the ministry in Ephesians 4:11. Don't most jobs leave their employees tired after several hours? This is because it is work.

Another thing that you will expend is money. Does it not cost you money to go to work everyday? Do you not spend money at work for lunch everyday?

It is the same thing with the work of ministry. **You will spend some of your money in order to do the work.** Someone may say, "In the case of secular work, we expend money but we get some back at the end of the month." Dear friend, your rewards and treasures will come one day in Heaven!

> But lay up for yourselves TREASURES IN HEAVEN...
>
> **Matthew 6:20**

I do not believe in giving money to lay people to help them to pay for their transportation when visiting sheep. Do not give money to lay musicians, lay shepherds or lay pastors to help them come to church. When they were ordinary church members weren't they spending money to come to church? If you start paying laymen, it will soon become as though you were hiring people to do a part-time job.

**Very often when you pay people, their attitude changes and it becomes more of, "Is this all I get for my hard work?"** I have decided to let the Lord pay those who work for Him. Make no mistake about this. Praying, visiting, counselling and interacting with people is hard work. As you do this work you will expend your energy and money. When you begin to feel tired, just remember it is a sign that you are really *working for God*.

## 4.  Ministry work is repetitive and regular

By nature, all real work is repetitive and regular. If the ministry is "work", then it will have features which make it *repetitive and regular*. Sometimes you may be bored but you just have to keep on doing the "work" - praying, visiting, counselling and interacting (PVCI).

Many pastors don't pray much because they feel it's repetitive and boring. But when prayer becomes your work you will have to repeat your prayers and you will have to pray regularly. When visiting becomes your work, you will have to visit repeatedly and regularly.

There is a difference between a social visit to a friend's house and a pastoral visit. **Pastoral visits must be conducted repeatedly by shepherds. Shepherds must intentionally go to the homes of their members on a regular basis.**

No one ever told me what to do in ministry. I have naturally wanted to pray, to visit and to counsel my people. Now that our church is much larger I feel deprived when I am not able to know all of my sheep personally.

I struggle to know their names and to remember who they are. But it is almost an impossible task! I wish I knew all of their homes.

I wish I could attend all of their important family events. It is a natural desire. **Anyone who is a true pastor has what I call 'natural care' and does not need to be supervised!**

Don't we all go to work when we don't feel like it? Don't we all go to the same work place repeatedly and regularly although we don't feel like it? In the same way, anyone who claims to be doing the work of the ministry must rise up and repeatedly do the important tasks of a shepherd. We don't pray just because we feel like it. We pray because we have to! We must rise up early and intercede for the people God has given us.

## 5.  Ministry work is supervised or unsupervised work

> Go to the ant... and BE WISE: Which HAVING NO
> GUIDE, OVERSEER, OR RULER,  Provideth her
> meat...
>
> Proverbs 6:6-8

All work falls into two categories: supervised work or unsupervised work.  There are therefore two classes of working shepherds: those who need supervision and people who do not need supervision.

**In every field, the supervised person is paid less than the unsupervised person!**  Decide to be a shepherd who does not need to be told what to do, when to pray, and whom to counsel.  Your rewards in heaven will be even greater.

From today, decide that no one will ever have to supervise you to pray, read the Bible, study, visit or any such thing.  Just do your work without supervision.  Be a pastor who does not need supervision.

Nobody tells me that I have to pray.  I know I have to pray, so I just pray.  Become a shepherd who naturally (without supervision) cares about the work of God.  Be like Timothy.  Paul said that there was no one like him.  He had a natural "care" for the sheep.  He didn't need to be told what to do.  It just came naturally.  I believe that is the heart of a true pastor.

> But I trust in the Lord Jesus to send Timotheus...  For
> I have no man likeminded, who will NATURALLY
> CARE for your state.
>
> Philippians 2:19, 20

No one ever told me what to do in ministry.  I have naturally wanted to pray, do visit and to counsel my people.  Now that our church is much larger, I feel deprived when I am not able to know all my sheep personally.

I struggle to know their names and to remember who they are.  But it is almost an impossible task!  I wish I knew all their homes. I wish I could attend all their important family events. It is a natural desire. **Anyone who is a true pastor has what I call natural care and does not need to be supervised.**

From today, decide that no one will ever have to supervise you to pray, read the Bible, study, visit or any such thing. Just do your work without supervision. Be a pastor who does not need supervision.

## Chapter 11

# Seven Ministries of "Poimen"

In this chapter, I want to show you a very important revelation concerning all of the ministry offices. Each office of the Body of Christ; apostle, prophet, evangelist, pastor and teacher, has several different ministries under it. A pastor will have several ministries operating under his office. A prophet will also have different ministries operating under his office. For example, a minister standing in the office of a prophet will primarily function in the ministry of preaching and teaching. Beware of so-called prophets who do not preach the Word of God but only give personal prophecies.

However, let it be very clear that anything that does not put the Word of God in its proper place is doomed to failure with the passage of time. In the beginning was the *Word*... Let the *Word* of Christ dwell in you richly... Thy *Word* is a light unto my path... Thy entrance of thy *Word* giveth light... Anything without the *Word* is in darkness and is not of God.

## The Office of a Prophet Has Ministries Under it

All offices of the ministry have a primary function of teaching and preaching. The Word comes first and is of paramount importance in every ministerial office. After this, a prophet may operate in the ministry of healing, and other revelation gifts like "word of knowledge" and "word of wisdom". The prophet may also flow in the ministry of predictive prophesying or exhortative prophesying. From Scripture, you will see that Jesus was a great prophet. His principal ministry was to go about preaching and teaching the Word of God. Jesus, the prophet, also had a healing ministry.

**...and they glorified God, saying, That a GREAT PROPHET is risen up among us...**

**Luke 7:16**

**And Jesus went about all the cities and villages, TEACHING in their synagogues, and PREACHING the gospel...**

**Matthew 9:35**

**How God anointed Jesus... who went about doing good, and HEALING all that were oppressed of the devil...**

**Acts 10:38**

Jesus, the prophet, operated in the gifts of revelation. Standing in the office of a prophet, he ministered to the woman of Samaria; The woman of Samaria immediately realized she had met someone standing in the office of a prophet. Look at her response to Jesus' ministration.

**For thou hast had five husbands; and he whom thou now hast is not thy husband...**

**John 4:18**

**The woman saith unto him, Sir, I PERCEIVE THAT THOU ART A PROPHET.**

**John 4:19**

Jesus also operated in the ministry of predictive prophesying. In Matthew 24 he predicted the destruction of Solomon's temple (70 AD) when Jerusalem was destroyed by the Romans. Speaking of the temple he said, ...There shall not be left here one stone upon another..." (Matthew 24:2). Jesus gave extensive predictions concerning the end of the world. We would do well to take note of these prophecies because Jesus was a great prophet.

I have used the office of a prophet to illustrate how different ministries flow from one office in the church. Just as there is one Holy Spirit with different operations, manifestations and administrations, there can be one office with different ministries emanating from it. Let us now study the different ministries that flow from the office of the pastor (poimen).

# The Office of a Pastor (poimen) Has Ministries Under it

It is important that shepherds flow in all aspects of the ministry. God does not want an imbalance in ministry. A false balance is abomination to the Lord..." (Proverbs 11:1).

We may naturally flow in certain areas but be weaker in others. It is important to develop your weak areas so that you have a balanced ministry. Every profession has a symbol. The symbol of the medical profession is a staff with a snake around it.

The symbol of a king is a sceptre. The symbol of a shepherd is a staff. For example, a soldier's symbol is a rifle. It symbolizes his ability to kill and to destroy. By studying the symbol of the shepherd, we can see more clearly the different ministries of the pastor.

**The Lord is my shepherd... thy ROD and thy STAFF they comfort me.**

**Psalm 23:1, 4**

# The Seven Ministries of Poimen

## 1. The Ruling Ministry

**And out of his mouth goeth a sharp sword... and he shall rule them with a ROD OF IRON...**

**Revelation 19:15**

The first ministry of a pastor is the ruling ministry. The traditional perception of a pastor is of someone who is soft, kind-hearted, compassionate, poorly paid, available at all times, and a never-complaining doormat. This picture is not one of a ruler but rather a picture of one who is ruled. I believe that a pastor must be kind-hearted and patient, but one of his cardinal roles is to lead and to rule. A pastor is the head of the local church. A head must take decisions.

**The Lord is my shepherd... HE LEADETH ME beside the still waters.**

**Psalm 23:1, 2**

A true shepherd leads sheep to the place where they need to go. You cannot be a good leader if you are weak. Every church needs a strong voice that is confident and bold in the Lord. The sheep are looking for someone with direction, who knows where he is going. A pastor must lead the people spiritually and in other areas such as in the family and social dimensions.

When the church does not have a strong capable leader, something is wrong. You may be surprised to discover what the prophet Isaiah described as a curse.

**When a man shall take hold of his brother of the house of his father, saying, Thou hast clothing, BE THOU OUR RULER, and let this ruin be under thine hand: In that day shall he swear, saying, I will not be an healer; for in mine house is neither bread nor clothing: MAKE ME NOT A RULER of the people.**

**Isaiah 3:6, 7**

It is a curse to have weak and spineless leadership. Learn to speak to your sheep with authority. When I say authority I do not mean you should dominate their lives. Lead them with a high level of confidence and control. Sheep are meant to be led.

You have authority over the sheep God has placed in your care. You will answer for their souls one day.

**A leader who refuses to take important decisions is doomed to failure.**

**A good leader takes decisions when all necessary information has come to him!** These decisions may be hard and painful. If you, as the shepherd do not take them your church is doomed to wither.

Just look around and see how many churches are dead and lifeless. They are a far cry from what their founders had envisaged. This is often because as wrong things began to creep in, the leaders were afraid to rock the boat and take important decisions. Things will get out of hand.

Sometimes when I look at some hopelessly incompetent government corporations and agencies, I just marvel. They make huge losses, and generate a lot of waste in the system. I have been to government offices where I see everyone reading newspapers. Sometimes you see twenty secretaries in one office with one typewriter. They have nothing to do, yet they are paid with the taxpayers' money every month. What a pity! They sleep, eat and chat all day. Their managers are afraid to take the decision that nineteen out of the twenty typists must be laid off.

The country becomes poorer and poorer and people wonder why. The reason is simple. The leaders have refused to assess the situation and take a strong but hard decision. They are refusing to rule. The fear of losing political power makes democratic leaders become liars and hypocrites.

I am not afraid of taking such decisions because I realize that the church will deteriorate if I do not. I teach pastors to remove stagnating leaders and replace them with willing and capable workers. I make the necessary changes in my staff and with my shepherds when I realize a change must be made.

Don't be afraid of changes. Sometimes, it is only a big change that will lead to a big breakthrough. **A minor transformation will take place when you take minor decisions. But a *major* transformation will occur when you are bold enough to take a *major* decision.** Be a strong ruler and lead your sheep to green pastures.

Lady pastors can learn to be strong firm leaders without being ill-natured and quarrelsome. Lady shepherds should be gentle and effective, without being cantankerous.

# 2. The Way-Making Ministry

**And the Lord said unto Moses... But LIFT THOU UP THY ROD, and stretch out thine hand over the sea, and divide it: and the children of Israel shall go on dry ground through the midst of the sea.**

**Exodus 14:15, 16**

As a leader, God will tell you to speak to his people, giving them many instructions. There is something I call the *Way-Making Ministry*. After you have given instructions to the sheep, help them to obey the Word. A true shepherd loves his sheep and tries to help them to obey God.

Moses was the shepherd of the people of Israel. His instructions were to cross the Red Sea. After receiving that command he stretched forth his rod and made a way where there was no way. That is what I call the way-making ministry of the pastor.

**Every shepherd must learn to make a way where there seems to be no way for the people of God.**

When some of your sheep think that their house is too far away from the church, go and visit them at whichever corner they live. This will prove to them that their homes are not too far.

## My Visit Produced a Pastor

I knew a family that lived about a two-hour train ride from one of our churches. When I called them, they said it was too far to attend church. So one Saturday, I took a car and together with another pastor, we drove all the way to their house. They were so surprised to see us visiting them. This is one thing that visits do. It establishes the fact that people are not too far for me to visit them. From that day, the entire family decided to come to church, taking the train and travelling two hours to church.

They did this for a number of years, and today one of them is a pastor in our church. Make a way for your sheep. Help them to see that it is possible to obey the Word of God. Sometimes when they don't have money, tell them to come to church and give them some money to help them attend. You may not be able to give them money all of the time, but the fact that you did it once or twice encourages them and shows that you really care. This is the pastor's heart.

## Make a Way for Marriage

As a pastor, you often see that your sheep are looking for husbands or wives. Don't just look on unconcerned and preach about how good it is to be married. Discuss the practical concerns of choosing a partner with them. Help them to notice one another. I call that Shepherdorial Linking.

Teach your members that they can find a good partner within the church. Some people may not like that idea, but it works and stabilizes the sheep. Of course, do not force people to marry each other; you should not guarantee them happiness if they choose someone you have recommended. Marriage is very complicated and they may curse you for the rest of their lives for influencing them to marry someone. They will think to themselves, "I would never have married this person. It was pastor who made me marry her."

## Make a Way for Employment

I preach to my members about prosperity and about how they should work. After I've done that, the way-making anointing comes upon me and I help them to get jobs. If one of my church members is strategically positioned as an employer, I would speak to them about a sheep who needs employment. Sometimes a person you have recommended will disgrace you. But do not let that deter you from making a way for other good sheep.

**It is not good enough to say "Cross the Red Sea"; you must make a way for them to cross!**

# Make a Way for People to Attend

I have often changed meeting times or rehearsal times just so that one person could attend. I am a pastor and I want all of my sheep to attend the meetings. Schedule reasonable meeting times. *Make things convenient for people.* That is the way-making ministry in action.

Schedule fewer meeting times without compromising the number of meetings. Sunday is a good time to meet and counsel your sheep. For example, when a person already has a service he attends, you can always combine it with another meeting; don't let him travel to church twice when he could do it once.

**Be an expert at overcoming the excuses of church members.** When they say that church services are too long, point out to them how many hours they spend watching video. When they say that the church is too far from their homes, ask them how far their jobs are from their homes. When the church member doesn't have shoes, get him a pair. Be a way-maker.

# 3. The Territory-Taking Ministry

The territory-taking ministry of a pastor is embodied in his vision. If the pastor is a visionary, he will always want to take more territory for Christ. **The way you can take more territory for God is through prayer and fasting.** A pastor must lead his sheep into spiritual warfare.

I always have a new vision for my church. When I had twenty members, I had a vision to have fifty. When I had fifty people at the Korle Bu Teaching Hospital, I dreamed of the day when I would see a hundred people sitting in church on Sunday morning.

When I had five hundred, I dreamt of a thousand. It is the duty of the pastor to dream about greater territories for the kingdom of God. We are not a social club. We are not fighting a psychological warfare. We are into spiritual warfare.

> **And Moses said unto Joshua, Choose us out men, and go out, fight with Amalek: tomorrow I will stand on the top of the hill with the ROD OF GOD in mine hand. And it came to pass, when Moses held up his hand, that Israel prevailed: and when he let down his hand, Amalek prevailed.**
>
> **Exodus 17:9, 11**

People who take new territories are people who fast and pray. I believe in praying for long periods. I believe in fasting as the Spirit leads. Moses, the shepherd of God's people, stretched out his rod in warfare against Amalek. **Moses' rod symbolized the power of intercessory prayer.** It is the art of travailing in prayer for the ministry.

What you see happening in the physical is only a manifestation of what has taken place in the spiritual realm.

Anyone who calls himself a pastor must learn to fight with prayer in the realm of the spirit. If you want to have a big church, you must learn to fight for it in the spiritual realm. Every physical territory is occupied by evil spirits who dominate the area.

**Africa is dominated by territorial spirits of poverty, superstition and war.** That is why the continent, although blessed with human and natural resources, is plagued with backwardness and under-development.

**Europe is dominated by territorial spirits of atheism, homosexuality, and immorality.** That is why there are ministers who are homosexual and millions who do not believe in God. There are even gay clubs within churches now.

This is the return of Sodom and Gomorrah! It certainly signals imminent destruction.

Any shepherd who wants to do the work of the ministry will come face to face with the territorial spirits of that area. When I travel from place to place, I can virtually feel the difference in the spiritual atmosphere. When I am in Ghana, I sense a lighter and easier spiritual climate than when I am in a place like Switzerland.

Develop the art of intercession for taking more territories for God. That means you must develop several important prayer skills.

# Four Important Prayer Skills for Effective Intercession

## 1. The art of praying alone for several hours

Jesus did that! If we want to have the results that he had we must use the methods he used.

**And it came to pass, as he was ALONE PRAYING, his disciples were with him...**

**Luke 9:18**

## 2. The art of leading people into long hours of advancement prayer

Whenever we have fasting and long hours of prayer, I often lead the church myself. I do not delegate it to anybody. Sometimes we have prayer meetings from 8 o'clock in the morning until 8 o'clock in the evening. Teach people to pray in tongues for hours, it is a very important practice.

Many times, I take my pastoral staff to the mountains to wait on God. We pray from morning until evening every day until we return. Jesus often took his disciples to the Garden of Gethsemane.

**And he came out, and went, as he was wont, [as his custom was] to the mount of Olives; and his disciples also followed him. AND WHEN HE WAS AT THE PLACE, HE SAID UNTO THEM, PRAY...**

**Luke 22:39, 40**

Lead your church to pray for church growth. Lead your sheep to ask God for increase. There are many ways that the increase will benefit all of the church members. So tell them that it is for their own good to take new territories for Christ.

3.  **The art of praying with the spirit and with your understanding**

In 1 Corinthians 14:15, Paul asked a question, "What is it then? I will pray with the spirit and I will pray with the understanding also."

He also said, "I thank my God, I speak with tongues more than ye all." (1 Corinthians 14:18). The apostle was very happy about exercising the gift of tongues but he also prayed with his understanding.

In taking new territories, you must learn both aspects of the prayer weapon. Praying in tongues is a powerful tool to defeat the enemy. Use it and spend hours speaking in the spirit concerning your future and your ministry. Pray with the understanding also. As you pray with your understanding, you will find yourself praying out the prophetic for your life. You will find yourself speaking words of faith concerning church growth and ministry.

I can pray continuously with my understanding for several hours, if necessary. **Today, there are many Christians who cannot pray for more than one minute with their understanding.** They can only pray in tongues. It is a sign that they are shallow and don't really know God.

Every pastor must be able to stand up and pray for at least one hour in their understanding.

I remember when I was in Geneva praying for church growth. I remember praying with my understanding for long periods. It was a powerful time of fighting the devil and taking territory for God.

4.  **The art of travailing in prayer**

There is something called travailing prayer. It is the art of prayer that results in the giving birth of a new spiritual baby. It may be a baby church, it may be a new Christian, it may be a new ministry, it may be a new fellowship.

It may even involve the giving birth to a mature Christian from a baby Christian. The Apostle Paul travailed twice for the Christians in Galatia. The first time was to give birth to the Galatian church. The second time was to give birth to a Christ-like maturity in the church.

**My little children, of whom I travail in birth again until Christ be formed in you...**

**Galatians 4:19**

How will you know that you are practicing travailing (birth-giving) prayer? It is very simple. Until your prayers have begun to resemble what happens in the labor ward, you have not begun to pray travailing (birth-giving) prayers.

Let me give you three characteristics of travailing prayer.

**...Shall the earth be made to bring forth in one day? or shall a nation be born at once? for AS SOON AS ZION TRAVAILED, SHE BROUGHT FORTH her children.**

**Isaiah 66:8**

a.   Long hours

Women in labour spend hours and sometimes days in the labour ward trying to give birth to a new baby. You cannot claim that a three-minute prayer is travailing prayer. Nobody gives birth to a baby in three minutes. When you pray travailing prayers, you will give birth to a bigger church, new ministries and new things in God.

b.   Suffering and shame

Every normal woman suffers in the process of having a baby. That is why it is called a labour ward and not a playing ward. It is a ward of struggles and pain.

One day in 1988, I had an experience in the labor ward. I was a medical student who was assigned to deliver at least twenty-three babies. That night I was hoping to catch a couple more babies. I was sitting on a chair when a woman in labour came up behind me and gripped my shoulder, shouting, "Doctor, when? Doctor, when?"

I turned round to see who it was. To my surprise, here was a stark naked woman in labor. She was walking around the ward to help ease her pain. She was in such pain that she could not be bothered about wearing clothes or anything like that. She felt no shame at all and neither did many of the women on the labour ward. I realized this woman was struggling and agonizing for a new life to come into this world. **Dear friend, labour involves pain, suffering and shame.** It is no joke. Travailing prayer is just the same, it involves both pain and suffering.

Another form of suffering comes when you fast. Fasting is not easy. The only part of fasting I enjoy is the breaking of the fast. It is so nice to break a fast. However, fasting is part of the Christian experience. Paul said that he fasted often.

**...in hunger and thirst, in FASTINGS OFTEN...**
**2 Corinthians 11:27**

You may lose weight and people may ask you whether you are sick. One time, someone asked me if I thought I would enter heaven by being a skeleton. I was so skinny because I fasted so much. Yet, that didn't prevent me from getting a good wife. The anointing is more powerful than good looks!

c.  Hunger and tiredness

Christians want everything easy. The Bible says that whatsoever a man sows he will also reap. Travailing prayer will make you tired.

**Epaphras... always labouring fervently for you in prayers...**
**Colossians 4:12**

Epaphras was a labourer. He toiled in prayer. He labored in prayer for the Colossian church. When women deliver babies they are often hungry and tired. It is natural to be hungry and tired after hours of hard work. Do not tell me that your ten-minute prayer is something that can make you hungry and tired. Do not tell me that your ten-minute prayer is travailing prayer. It is not!

After many hours of labor and suffering you can expect to have something tangible in your hand. Every woman looks forward to that baby. That is why it is such a terrible experience for a woman to go to the labor ward and to come back without a baby. Expect a new baby of ministry in your life. The Word of God cannot be broken. If you are not prepared to travail in prayer then you are not prepared to have your baby.

**They that sow in tears shall reap in joy. He that goeth forth and weepeth, bearing precious seed, shall doubtless come again with rejoicing...**

**Psalm 126:5, 6**

Under the ministry of Jesus, we see travailing prayer in action. To every success story there are hours of hidden preparatory work that no one sees. People marveled at Jesus' ministry.

They said, "Never man spake like this man." (John 7:46). They glorified God saying, "We never saw it on this fashion." (Mark 2:12). Multitudes were converted under his ministry. The big question in town was, "Whence hath this man this wisdom, and these mighty works?" (Matthew 13:54). The secret of Jesus Christ's ministry was long private prayer times.

**...he went out into a mountain to pray, and continued ALL NIGHT in prayer to God.**

**Luke 6:12**

**...A GREAT WHILE BEFORE DAY, he went out, and departed into a solitary place, and there prayed.**

**Mark 1:35**

Even when multitudes thronged him (His church was growing, the crowds were there) and when he became famous, he still made time to pray alone.

**But so much the more went there a fame abroad of him: and great multitudes came together to hear, and to be healed by him of their infirmities. And HE WITHDREW HIMSELF into the wilderness, AND PRAYED.**

**Luke 5:15, 16**

Sometimes when he had friends around him, he would send them away and pray.

**And when he had SENT THEM AWAY, he departed into a mountain to pray.**

**Mark 6:46**

Decide to pray like Jesus prayed. I laugh to myself when people say I am a strategist. Many people think I am just a good administrator - that is why my church is growing. I know some people who think I do not pray much. It is sad when a person has a good administration it is assumed that he is not prayerful.

# 4. The Comforting Ministry

**...thy rod and thy staff they comfort me.**

**Psalm 23:4**

One of the principal ministries of a shepherd is to comfort the sheep. Every sheep should be able to say to his shepherd, "Your rod and your staff comfort me." Some people do not know why their churches do not grow.

The shepherd must genuinely love the sheep and care for them when they are in trouble. Never lose the opportunity to be by your sheep's side in their time of difficulty. The duty of the shepherd is to stand by his sheep in the time of their greatest need and greatest joy. It is not an option! Remember that, **sorrow shared is half sorrow, and joy shared is double joy.**

The sheep want to share their sorrows and their joy with their shepherd.

It is the duty of the shepherd to comfort the sheep. The comforting ministry starts by showing interest in things that are important to the sheep. Be interested in all of their major events; especially the birth of a child, marriages, sickness and funerals. God expects you to be there!

What is important to your sheep must be important to you. If you claim to be a pastor, what are you doing to show real love to your sheep?

Shepherds, if you do not genuinely love your people, they will not respond to your preaching. The Bible says that God is angry with the shepherds because they have not ministered to the sheep under the comforting ministry.

**The diseased have ye not strengthened, neither have ye healed that which was sick, neither have ye bound up that which was broken, neither have ye brought again that which was driven away, neither have ye sought that which was lost; but with force and with cruelty have ye ruled them.**

**Ezekiel 34:4**

The sheep often know the Word before you preach. What they want is some love. Everybody responds to love. It is only demons that cannot be loved! Remember that love never fails. The Bible does not say, "Preaching never fails" or, "Teaching never fails". The Bible says "Love never fails". The comforting ministry is love in action.

## 5. The Measurement Ministry

One of the principal duties of a shepherd is to do what I call measuring the temple. Measuring the temple helps you to know where you stand.

**And there was given me a reed like unto a rod: and the angle stood, saying, Rise, and MEASURE the temple of God, and the altar, and them that worship therein.**
**Revelation 11:1**

This involves a critical analysis of the way things are going. Pastors need to take time off to analyze themselves and to see whether things are being done according to the call of God and the vision God gave.

The first thing you must constantly measure is yourself. Ask yourself, "Am I doing what God called me to do?" The reason why I am writing books now is because I believe it is in obedience to the ministry God gave me to teach His Word. No matter what additional ministry I have, I am constantly trying to fulfil the call of God on my life according to his specifications.

Even when I had over fifty churches to oversee, my self-analysis (measurement ministry) made me see that I had to keep on pastoring the church and teaching the Wor d of God. If pastors and ministers were to analyze their ministry, it would help them to take important decisions.

## Only Twenty-five Members after Twelve Years

I was chatting with a pastor who had been in the ministry for twelve years. After being in the ministry for twelve years, he only had twenty-five members in his church. His church was in a city where there are many large churches. By analyzing the reality of the situation, this pastor would have been helped to take an important decision for his life and ministry.

Surely, after some years there must be some growth. Anything that is alive and healthy grows naturally. If this pastor were to analyze his ministry, he may conclude that perhaps he was supposed to be an assistant and not the head. Perhaps he had to learn something new. Perhaps he needed to even close down the church. Analysis is very important in ministry.

## He Returned to the Ministry

Some years ago, I spoke to a pastor friend of mine. I had known this pastor for several years. He had been actively pastoring a church in a large city of the world.

Due to circumstances beyond his control, he found himself in another city. There he just attended a dead church. He was no longer actively involved in the ministry. He was just a church attendee.

I spoke to him and said, "If you are called of God to the ministry, then wherever you are and whatever your circumstance you must fulfil your ministry." I impressed upon him to analyze his condition (measuring ministry) as a pastor and take the important decisions that would bring him to a place where he was fulfilling his divine call. I'm happy to say that he did. Today, he is pastoring and overseeing many churches.

> **EXAMINE YOURSELVES, whether ye be in the faith; prove your own selves...**
> **2 Corinthians 13:5**

In other words, examine yourselves to see whether you are within your call and whether there is anything that you have to change. Can you imagine if the Mercedes-Benz car that is being sold today was exactly the same as it was fifteen years ago? It would be a very different car. The Mercedes-Benz of today is still a Benz but it is a much improved version of the 1950 model. That is how our churches and ministries must be - *continually upgraded and improved.*

We must compare what we are doing to what is in the Bible. **If you see something in the Bible that is not in your church, strive to attain that biblical standard.** I always marvel at people who fight against miracles and prophecies. The entire Bible is full of testimonies of supernatural and spectacular miracles.

If you have no miracles in your church please do not say that the day of miracles has passed. Just work on yourself until you have the miraculous operating through your ministry.

If people helped the poor in the Bible days, strive to have a church which ministers to the poor. Do not say that people who minister to the poor do so because they do not have anointing to win souls. Accept the fact that it is a biblical standard that you must attain! It is because we don't measure what we are doing, that we continue in the wrong thing for a long time.

Ask yourselves, "Am I a good person?" Ask your wife or husband what he thinks about your character. Ask yourself, "How many should we be at this stage?" Measure your performance and analyze your duties! Don't be like a husband or wife who appears so glorious on the outside. They call each other "sweetheart" and "honey" in public, but are brewing a stormy divorce at home. If you assess and judge yourself, God will not have to deal with you.

**But he that is spiritual judgeth all things, yet he himself is judged of no man.**

**1 Corinthians 2:15**

# 6. The Ministry of Correction

**...SHALL I COME UNTO YOU WITH A ROD, or in love, and in the spirit of meekness?**

**1 Corinthians 4:21**

Some people think that the pastor must be so soft that he cannot point out evil and correct it. The worst type of pastor is the one who cannot correct things that are going out of line. It is important to purge out certain tendencies from the flock. When your sheep realize that you are a weak leader, they will take you for a ride.

## Black Beauty

Many years ago, I went for a ride on a horse called Black Beauty. This was at Burma Camp, a military riding school in the city of Accra. I was a new rider; and the horse soon realized that I was a novice. Our instructor would take us on a ride through various fields in the countryside.

When we got to the boundary of the riding school, the horse didn't feel like going out for the ride so it stopped at the gate. I had a whip in my hand so I hit the horse several times and the horse began to kick and jump. It knew that I was afraid of it. Some of the more experienced riders in the group came along and encouraged me to put the horse in line and bring it out of the school and into the field. Would you believe that the horse calmly turned around and took me back to the stable? It utterly refused to go out on a ride that afternoon. I would say that the horse rode me, I didn't ride it!

Some months later after I became experienced, this horse was no match for me. I could make it do anything I wanted it to do. That is how the pastor must be with his sheep. If the people you are leading feel that you are weak, they will go out of line and do wrong things. When they realize that you are strong, they will stay in check.

Identify disloyal people and remove them from the fold. Rebuke people publicly when you have to.

## A Pastoral Introduction?

I remember during a Tuesday night service, my associate pastor called to the stage a church member who was notorious for stealing. The boy probably thought he was going to be introduced to the church. However, the pastor announced to the church that this young man was a dangerous thief who was going about taking things from church members. He went on to say that everybody in the church should be careful of him and not believe his lies anymore.

The church was dead calm for a second and then suddenly burst out in thunderous applause. This young man thought that he could take us for granted. He thought that because we are a church we would allow him to do anything he wanted. That was his mistake! The sheep will appreciate your strong leadership.

**...Know ye not that a little leaven leaventh the whole lump? Purge out therefore the old leaven...**

**1 Corinthians 5:6, 7**

To some of the sheep, you must be gentle and say things like:

"I am disappointed in you."

"I wasn't expecting this from you."

"I was expecting something better from you."

"Let this never happen again."

"Shame on you."

"I give you 20% for your Christianity."

**And of some have compassion, making a difference:**
**Jude 22**

Correcting the sheep does not mean you should disgrace them. You can correct them without disgracing them. If you do not correct them, that thing will begin to spread among the congregation.

## The "Ruby, Walk Out!" (RWO) Treatment

To some of the sheep, you must be rough and hard. With others, you must actually dismiss them from the church. I remember one pastor who stood in the pulpit and looked at two giggling girls and shouted from the pulpit, "Ruby, Walk Out!" She had no choice but to walk out, never to return.

**Cast out the scorner, and contention shall go out; yea,**
**strife and reproach shall cease.**
**Proverbs 22:10**

I call this the RWO treatment. Some people need to be dismissed from the church. Their presence in the church is not desirable or helpful, so get rid of them. It's as simple as that!

## 7. The Feeding Ministry

The importance of the feeding ministry of a shepherd cannot be overemphasized. It is a principal duty of a shepherd to feed his sheep. Everything else comes after he has done this principal duty. The authority to lead is given to those with the ability to feed.

> **FEED THY PEOPLE WITH THY ROD, the flock of thine heritage, which dwell solitarily in the wood, in the midst of Carmel: let them feed in Bashan and Gilead, as in the days of old.**
>
> **Micah 7:14**

I have people in my church who are older and wiser than I am in many respects. Yet in the church, I am their leader and I minister to them. Where would I get the authority to advise someone who could be my father or my mother? This authority is found in the ability to feed.

Where does your earthly father get his authority to tell you to come home or what to do with your life? It comes from the fact that he has fed you for years and continues to feed you. When your parents no longer feed you, the authority they have over your life drastically reduces.

Jesus said to Peter three times, "Feed my sheep". It is very important to the Lord that His sheep are well fed on the Word of God.

> **...Jesus saith unto him, Feed my sheep.**
>
> **John 21:17**

The principal duty of all ministry offices is to preach and to teach the Word of God.

> **And Jesus went about all the cities and villages, TEACHING in their synagogues, and PREACHING the gospel of the kingdom...**
>
> **Matthew 9:35**

Paul was an apostle and a prophet. He called himself an apostle to the Gentiles.

> **Paul, AN APOSTLE of Jesus Christ by the will of God... Whereunto I am appointed a PREACHER, and an apostle, and a TEACHER of the Gentiles.**
>
> **2 Timothy 1:1, 11**

It should be clear to every minister that our main resolve is to preach and teach the Word. What did Paul tell Timothy? Paul predicted that a time would come when people would not want the Bible to be preached.

> **I charge thee therefore before God, and the Lord Jesus Christ...PREACH THE WORD...For the time will come when they will not endure sound doctrine; but after their own lusts they shall heap to themselves teachers, having itching ears; And they shall turn away their ears from the truth, and shall be turned unto fables.**
>
> **2 Timothy 4:1-4**

Today, many people prefer to receive a prophecy. They want a quick, "bless me" prayer and some anointing with oil. **Pastors! Develop your ability to feed and to preach. It is your greatest asset.** Look around you and observe the great men of God you know. You will soon discover that every successful man of God has a strong ability to deliver the Word. Because this is so important, I am going to devote the whole of the next chapter to developing the art of preaching and teaching.

## *Chapter 12*

# How to Develop Your Ability to Preach and Teach

A pastor's greatest asset is his ability to preach and teach. Pastors of large churches are usually good preachers. The sheep know where the grass is green so they go there to be fed. Many pastors who have small churches have not developed the art of preaching and teaching! The following are strategic thoughts on how to improve your feeding ministry.

## Twenty-nine Strategies for Developing Excellent Preaching and Teaching Skills

### 1.    Preach out of your heart.

Every good pastor and shepherd must be able to preach from his heart. Thank God for notes. I believe in notes, but they are just a guide. I preach from my heart all the time.

**Out of the depths have I cried unto thee, O Lord.**
                                                                  **Psalm 130:1**

If the thing is not in your heart, don't bother to say it. People notice when what you are saying does not come from your heart. The best preachers are "heart preachers" and not "note preachers".

### 2.    Preach extemporaneously.

Extemporaneous means informal, unrehearsed, impromptu and "off the cuff". If you want your preaching to be powerful, and if you want people to listen to you, then learn to preach "off-the-cuff".

The powerful sermons recorded in the books of Acts were unrehearsed and from the heart of Peter and Paul. When Peter stood to preach for three thousand to be saved, do you think he was preaching from his notes? He stood up and addressed the crowd from his heart without any preparation per se.

I believe that preparation takes place over a long time. It takes a long time for a message to go deep down into your heart.

Do you want to preach for three thousand to be saved?

Do you want to preach to five thousand? Then learn how to preach extemporaneously. Even when you have prepared notes, let the preparation be so deep that you hardly have to refer to these notes.

**When you were proposing to your fiancée, did you read from notes?** Of course not! You spoke from your heart! You were able to capture one woman! Capture many souls for Christ using the same strategy. Many women have used their charm to win the hearts of their husbands. Use the same charm to turn people to Christ.

### 3. Preach in a charismatic style.

To be charismatic means to be Holy Spirit inspired. Let your preaching be anointed! Learn to trust the Holy Spirit. Jesus said, "I will teach you what to say in that very hour." What Jesus said is true. I have experienced it very many times. Shepherds, never turn down a preaching appointment because of a short notice.

**Preach the word; be instant in season, out of season...**
**2 Timothy 4:2**

When you start preaching the anointing will flow. **Many times when I start preaching I don't feel anointed, but as I begin to flow I can feel the anointing rising.** Learn to trust the Holy Spirit even if it is contrary to your wonderfully prepared sermon notes.

### 4. Preach in an orderly fashion.

Orderly preaching means there is a pattern that your listeners can follow. When they can follow the train of thought, the congregation usually remembers the message. To do this you often have to write down a few points.

**Let all things be done decently and in order.**
**1 Corinthians 14:40**

Even when you are preaching under inspiration, there are usually two or three points that you are trying to stress. Learn to preach in a charismatic style even whilst using prepared notes! Let there be some order to what you are saying.

I believe in writing notes and preaching with points. It helps to establish otherwise vague ideas.

### 5.    Preach with emotion.

I believe that every shepherd must preach using his or her emotions as well. If your teaching is bland and emotionless, it will not appeal to anyone. Let your sheep feel your happiness, laughter, righteous anger and your excitement. **Your excitement is contagious and will pass on to the congregation.** Your expressionless and lifeless sermon is also contagious and will minister death.

### 6.    Vary the tone of your voice.

Vary the tone of your voice. Anyone who is serious about what he is saying would naturally bring some variation in the tone of voice. Anything that is monotonous (one tone) is boring.

Learn to imitate other people's voices as you preach! Your congregation will love it! People want to have something that is real. They want to hear something that is funny. They also want something that they can relate to. Do not say, "I am not that type of person." Paul said, "I am made all things to all men, that I might by all means save some" (1 Corinthians 9:22).6

### 7.    Learn to preach by closely following a good preacher.

In the natural, many women learnt how to cook by doing exactly what their mothers did in the kitchen. Their food tastes exactly like their mother's food. Initially, they just copied their mother's recipes. However, with time they may have developed their own variations to the recipe. Nevertheless, they essentially learnt how to cook by copying someone who already knew how to cook. It is that simple in the natural. When it comes to preaching, many ministers have all sorts of psychological difficulties with accepting this reality.

I have never attended a Bible school. I have never studied homiletics. In fact, I didn't even know what that word meant until recently. **I learnt how to preach by watching and listening to good preachers; and I am not ashamed to say so. It is a proven method of acquiring a skill.** Even in medicine, you learn surgery by watching, assisting and then doing it under supervision. That is how I train my pastors. I teach them to listen to messages and soak them in! This method has worked and is still working very well for me. "...Wisdom is justified of her children" (Matthew 11:19)!!

First, you must choose someone who preaches well who can be your mentor. **Then consciously soak in the messages until you unconsciously flow in his style and message.** Choose a style that works and a message that has worked. I learnt to preach by sitting at the feet of Kenneth E. Hagin and Fred Price for hours.

I had watched and listened to Fred Price so much that without knowing it I began to preach like him. I did not do this consciously. I just loved his messages so much that I soaked them in hundreds of times. *I now know that I was learning by observing.*

The disciples, Peter, James and John didn't even know that they had learned to preach, and heal the sick until after Jesus had left. Suddenly, Peter was thrown into a situation where he had to preach a biting sermon. He spoke to the Pharisees in the same biting way that Jesus did. Without realizing it, Peter had learnt how to preach by being with Jesus.

**Now when they saw the boldness of Peter and John, and perceived that they were unlearned and ignorant**

**men, they marvelled; and they took knowledge of
them, that THEY HAD BEEN WITH JESUS.**

**Acts 4:13**

## 8.    Preach about what people are thinking.

Many times Jesus knew what the people were thinking.  He
often preached against what they were thinking.  A good preacher
can sense what the people are thinking about

**...the Pharisees heard it, they said, This fellow doth
not cast out devils, but by Beelzebub the prince of the
devils.  And Jesus KNEW THEIR THOUGHTS, and
said [preached] unto them...**

**Matthew 12:24, 25**

Do not close your eyes when you are preaching.  Look at them
eyeball to eyeball!  Preach against any negative thoughts that
they may have!  Do not preach about anything that is irrelevant.
People must comment that your preaching is biting.

## 9.    Dress nicely and appropriately.

Always dress decently and properly.  Every pastor should
endeavour to look decent and business-like when ministering.
If you are a young preacher, it is important that you dress
appropriately.  Otherwise, you may be mistaken for a worthless
young man. *Your dressing can upgrade your youthful appearance
and make you acceptable before an elderly crowd.*

Female pastors must be extra careful!  Women have been
designed to be attractive to men.  Men are also attracted to
women. Therefore, lady pastors or female shepherds must ensure
that they do not put on any clothing that is revealing.

## 10.  Shave and trim your beard neatly.

Decide whether to be clean-shaven or to keep a beard.  If you
shave you must do it regularly.  If you decide to keep a beard, you
must keep it trim and neat.  Some people's beards have spittle all
over them.  Others have unidentified objects hanging in there!

At times, you may have to instruct a shepherd to shave off his beard because it looks too scruffy. Some Bible schools do not even allow students to keep a beard. The facts are that your beard changes your appearance completely.

### 11. Hair should be well kept.

Your hair sends messages to everyone. The lady pastors in particular must maintain their hair in good condition. Otherwise, people will feel, "If she can't even take care of her hair, can she take care of me?" Get a wig if you need one. A wig will always come in handy when you don't have time to do your hair. Don't look like a boy if you are a girl! Let your beauty help your ministry!

### 12. Develop appropriate gestures and posture.

Your gestures refer to your body movements during preaching. Observe any good preacher and you will notice that his preaching style includes many interesting gestures and postures. Your body movements add a lot to the message you are preaching. It keeps the congregation attentive. If you do not already use gestures, decide to consciously learn and add them to your preaching.

### 13. Vary the volume.

When preaching there are times when you must speak loudly. At other times, the preacher must shout! There are also moments when whispering is very effective.

Female ministers must be conscious of not shouting and screaming. This can be quite offensive. The shrill voice of a shrieking lady pastor is certainly not inspiring. Your high-pitched shriek may actually turn the attention of the congregation away from your message.

### 14. Move around freely.

At times you must stay behind the pulpit and preach. However, you must learn to move about when you are preaching. Sometimes it is good to walk into the crowd to get a feel of the atmosphere.

## 15. Congregational interaction.

I always involve the congregation when I preach. You must learn to involve your congregation by asking them questions. Occasionally call out some familiar names. It helps to keep everybody alert.

## 16. Eye contact.

When ministering look into the eyes of the people. **Jesus said that we should feed His sheep, not his giraffes!** Do not look above their heads, look into their eyes! See whether they are dead or alive! As a preacher, you must discern what they are thinking. Watch their facial expressions to know whether they understand what you are saying. Surprisingly, there are messages written all over their faces. You may even notice that people are asleep. This should prompt you to make your sermon less boring.

I once heard a true story about a church member who died sitting in his seat during a service. They called an ambulance to come and collect the dead man.

Upon the arrival of the ambulance, they found several congregation members asleep whilst the pastor was preaching. It was impossible for them to know who was asleep and who was dead. So they carried out several people only to find them waking up in the ambulance. The attendants weren't sure who was dead or not! Neither did the pastor know.

How does a pastor continue to preach to a congregation that is asleep or dead? If he was looking at their faces during his ministration he would have known when they died!

17. Your preaching must be relevant.

Your preaching must be relevant. It must be related to what is going on in the world around you. People must be able to say that your preaching is down-to-earth and easy to understand. Once the message loses its relevance, it loses its power. Jesus was very relevant.

**Or those eighteen, upon whom the tower in Siloam fell, and slew them, think ye that they were sinners above all men that dwelt in Jerusalem?**

**Luke 13:4**

When people were killed in an accident at the tower in Siloam He immediately spoke about it. He used it as an illustration for them to repent or likewise perish. That is what I call relevance.

Some people feel they must preach about complex things in order to impress people. Don't you know that the greatest people are simple people?

Why are you preaching about Aaron's beard? How is the color of Aaron's garments going to help the sheep? Please be relevant and practical!

### 18. You must have a command of current events.

Relate your preaching to current events that may be affecting the members in anyway. It helps them to relate to your preaching. Unemployment figures in Western Europe are of no interest to the average African. The conflict between North and South Korea is not even known by the average African. Use current events that are relevant to the people you are speaking to.

### 19. Use "windows" in your preaching.

Windows are illustrations, amusing stories and personal life testimonies that allow people to "see" into your sermon. A pastor who just reads out scripture after scripture without any real life explanation is just ministering death and not life. **A pastor who is not prepared to "open up" and tell people about himself and about his life will never be a good preacher.**

Ensure that you preach with windows. As soon as you begin to give them a story that explains the message, they will begin to understand. People especially love to hear things about your personal life. It is a window into your private life and everyone loves to peep. Church members cannot understand your sermon without the use of windows. Jesus preached with windows all the time. He continually used real life stories, parables and illustrations. I insist that all my pastors preach with windows! I insist on it because I believe it is one of the most important aspects of good preaching!

## 20. Laughter.

Develop the art of making people laugh. People want to be happy. There is so much sadness in the world that everyone looks forward to hope and happiness. People want to laugh, so make them laugh whilst you are preaching.

## 21. Soak in preaching tapes.

You must invest in preaching messages. Soak them in. Play them over and over again until you preach it exactly as it is, using your own illustrations and personal life stories. Soaking in the words of a man of God through CDs and videos imparts the anointing or spirit of that person into you.

**And the spirit entered into me when HE SPAKE unto me...**

**Ezekiel 2:2**

In John 6:63 Jesus said, "The words that I speak unto you, they are spirit, and they are life." This means that the more of Jesus' words you hear, the more "spirit" (anointing) comes into you.

The Bible says in Acts 10:44 that "While Peter yet spake these words, the Holy Ghost (the anointing) fell on all them which heard the word."

There is something within the word of the king called anointing. As you speak, the Holy Spirit will enter the spirit of the people.

## 22. Catch the anointing to teach.

As you soak in the tapes of a man of God, you will catch an anointing to minister. Your teaching and preaching ministry will improve.

It is "not by might, nor by power, but by my Spirit, saith the Lord of hosts." (Zechariah 4:6). The anointing makes the difference in ministry, not strategies and cunning ideas. Don't be too big to learn from someone else. We all learn from others. Ninety percent of what we know is learnt from somebody.

**23. Title your sermon.**

Titling your message gives you clarity of thought. The congregation will know that they are taking "something" home. Your message titles should usually stay within an average of a one-to-five worded catchy sentence. For e.g., Abrahamic Success, Divine Provision, Frugality, Can-Do Man, How to Develop your Potential. Occasionally you may have a long sentence topic, for instance: Twenty-five Reasons Why You Must Be a Permanent Member, Forty Reasons Why Some Christians Don't Pay Tithes. Titling your message helps people to understand what you are talking about.

**24. Preach with authority and confidence.**

People must feel that you know what you are preaching about. When people feel that you are not sure of what you are saying they will no longer receive your preaching. The thing that struck the Pharisees about Jesus' teaching was his authority.

**...By what authority doest thou these things? and who gave thee this authority?**

**Matthew 21:23**

**For he taught them as one having authority, and not as the scribes.**

**Matthew 7:29**

**25. Prepare extensively to preach.**

Preparation to minister does not take place a few minutes before a sermon is delivered. It takes place all the time. My preparation to minister is constant. Without long-term preparation, you can never really preach from your heart. Prayer is a vital part of your preparation. A pastor must spend Saturday evening to Sunday morning in prayer. Specifically pray for the following:

■    That everyone who came the week before will attend again.

■    That new people will attend church and be born again.

■    That there will be church growth.

■    That the flock will understand the Word and their lives will be affected.

■    That every need will be met: healing, peace of mind, salvation, deliverance.

■    That God would give you a spirit of revelation in the Word.

## 26.  Introduce your message as something important.

You must let your congregation know and feel that the message is important. If you tell them that you have a very important message to give to them, they will sit up and listen. Even before you begin ministering, you should inform them that this message is vital for their Christian life.

## 27.  Learn to preach in series.

One of the challenges of pastoral preaching and teaching is the challenge of having to preach to the same crowd of people each week. Church members expect the pastor to have a fresh and new revelation every week. Thank God for the Holy Spirit. Even if we are not capable, He is able.

I have discovered that pastoral preaching is best done in series. If part one is good, many people will come back to hear part two and part three. However, if every week you preach a different sermon, then there will be no motivation to continue receiving the lesson.

## 28.  End the message well.

Learn to conclude your messages well. End on a happy note. End when people are laughing. They will look forward to hearing more next time.

## 29.  Do altar calls for salvation and healing.

I believe every minister must consistently make altar calls for salvation.  This gives ordinary members the opportunity to practically give their lives to Christ.  Pastors and shepherds should not be afraid that no one will respond to your altar call.  After all you are not trying to impress anyone; you are trying to please God.  He wants all of His people to be saved.  I make altar calls at weddings, receptions, parties and anywhere else I find myself ministering.  I will use every opportunity I get.   Every pastor must learn to use strong persuasive and evangelistic language to draw out any sinner that might be present in the congregation.

## Chapter 13

# How to Be a Good Shepherd

There are good pastors and bad ones too. Are you going to be a good pastor? Are you going to be a good shepherd? The Bible says that whatsoever a man findeth to do, he should do it with all his might.

**Whatsoever thy hand findeth to do, do it with thy might...**

**Ecclesiastes 9:10**

If you are going to be a pastor, be a good one! Let us use the Word of God to show us exactly who a good pastor is. Some people think a good pastor is someone who is gentle and nice to people. Others think it is someone who is a very good preacher. What does the Word of God say? Who does Jesus say a good shepherd is? What is it like to be a good shepherd?

Jesus said He was a good shepherd. He spoke extensively about what a good shepherd does in the tenth chapter of John.

## Twelve Signs of a Good Shepherd

1.   **A good shepherd leads his sheep.**

**To him the porter openeth...and LEADETH THEM OUT.**

**John 10:3**

What does it mean to lead sheep? It means to be practically available for them to see and learn from you in every area of life and ministry. Anything you want your sheep to do, you must first do it yourself. They will follow you if they see you doing it first!

A pastor who wants his church members to pray must practically lead them into prayer. When the sheep see the shepherd taking the lead, they are convinced that the ground is safe and can follow confidently. Contrarily, a bad shepherd would sit at home and send the members to go for a prayer meeting alone.

I have always tried to do first, what I wanted my people to do. When we were building a basement in our church, we could not afford to hire the necessary machinery. We had to dig ourselves. I needed the help of the entire church to drill and dig very deep into the ground. After that, we needed to carry tons of red sand out of the pit.

I could have easily delegated it to some others, but I decided to dig and carry the sand myself. I believe my decision-motivated members of all social standings to get involved.

Students, lawyers, doctors and businessmen came out to carry sand like ordinary labourers. They worked with all their might. Why was that? They had seen their shepherd taking the lead.

I want you to notice something that made David popular.

> **But all Israel and Judah loved David, because he went out and came in before them.**
>
> **1 Samuel 18:16**

Why did the subjects of Israel love David? The answer is simple. They could see him practically going in and out with them and doing things with them.

We have a large attendance at our mid-week service. Many people are surprised that so many people attend church on a Tuesday evening. The fact is that I'm always there myself. I consider it an important meeting. The sheep see that, and follow my example.

Sometimes we have long periods of fasting with all-night prayer meetings everyday. You would be surprised to see how many people attend every night. I tell my members that I am struggling and suffering in the fast just like them, and they love to hear it. The sheep are always happy to identify with the shepherd when the shepherd identifies with them.

Leadership is very spiritual. Even when people do not see you physically, they follow you spiritually. I have found that sheep have a mysterious way of becoming like their shepherd. They are following him in the spirit!

## They Caught the Pastor's Anointing

Many years ago, there was a scandal in a large church. The senior pastor of the church had an affair with one of his members. The secret relationship had been ongoing until the lady became pregnant and exposed it. The Christian community was surprised! However, more surprises were to follow.

After the senior pastor finally admitted to his sin, it prompted a series of confessions from other pastors and leaders of the same church. Unknown to each other, the other pastors, leaders and sheep were all involved in similar sins.

One evening, the associate pastor announced to the congregation, "I have a confession to make. I am a womanizer. If anyone saw me coming from sister so-and-so's house in the morning... Whatever you thought happened, that is what happened. I am sorry to say that I have had affairs with four different girls in the church."

After this confession, many other immoral sins were exposed as being very common in the church.

A pastor is a spiritual leader over a flock. **What you do is what the people will do! They cannot rise above you unless you the leader show the way through righteous living.** That is why it is important for all shepherds to maintain very high standards.

Go ahead of your sheep. Do not operate as an executive, just walking in and out like a "big shot". There is no place for "big shots" in the harvest field. There is no place for "unreal leaders" in the real world of the sheep.

## 2.   A good shepherd knows his sheep by name.

**...and he calleth his own sheep by NAME...**
**John 10:3**

If you are a shepherd over a few people, you must know all their names. You must want to know their names and call them by name. Nobody is a number! Nobody wants to be called "Hey!" or "You there!"

You must get to know new people everyday. Keep asking their names until the name sticks. I am not ashamed of asking somebody his name seventy times until it sticks. When you know the sheep by name they cannot simply walk out on you.

## 3.   A good pastor is known by the sheep.

**...for they know his voice. And a stranger will they not follow...**
**John 10:4, 5**

How do people know the voice of the shepherd? How do you know the voice of someone? It is because you have heard them speak to you time and time again. A good shepherd must speak to his sheep over and over until they know his voice.

I preach to my church all the time. I do not often have guest speakers. I believe in guest speakers, but I believe the best person to preach to my sheep is me because I am their shepherd. I preach about ninety percent of the time.

When a woman gives birth to a baby, her breasts are full of milk for the new child. So it is with the shepherd. His spirit is full of the Word to give to his children. No other woman's body and breasts are better qualified to feed her own child. Nature made it that way. Because you gave birth, you are naturally primed up to feed what you have brought forth.

When your sheep are used to your voice, they will not follow strangers. If you call yourself a pastor, rise-up and feed your sheep regularly. **Preaching and teaching only becomes feeding when it is regular.** Preach to them all of the time, and teach them from your heart. They will grow and give birth to others.

They will know your voice on the issues of marriage, business, success and life in general. They will want to hear your voice concerning different aspects of their life. The voice of a true shepherd always rings in the spirit of his sheep. I question whether you are a real shepherd if you do not regularly and consistently feed your sheep.

**4.    A good pastor stays with the sheep.**

**The hireling fleeth, because he is an hireling, and careth not for the sheep.**

**John 10:13**

Anyone who calls himself a pastor will want to stay around and mingle with the members, talk with them and be interested in them. David said,

**One thing have I desired of the Lord, that will I seek after; THAT I MAY DWELL IN THE HOUSE OF THE LORD all the days of my life, to behold the beauty of the Lord, and to inquire in his temple.**

**Psalm 27:4**

David wanted to stay in the house of the Lord. He actually wanted to live there. And you want to rush home! Are you really called?

I question the genuineness of a pastor who has no interest in staying around for a while after service to mingle and chat with the sheep. The Bible says that the hireling flees. This means that he dashes off quickly! He wants to get away from the people!

Such people cannot stand visitors in their homes. They always say things like, "I need my privacy" or "I can't stand having all these people around" and "I can't cook for so many people". Remember that a bishop is supposed to be "given to hospitality" (1 Timothy 3:2).

I once knew a white minister and his wife who were pastoring a large church in a European city. It happened that many of the members of his church were Black people; some Ghanaians, some Nigerians, etc. One day, while having coffee with this pastor and his wife, I got a feeling from certain things they said, that they did not really like Black people. But it is important to like the people God has given to you as sheep.

It was no wonder that even though they had a large church, they one day abandoned the flock and went elsewhere.

### 5. A good shepherd knows his sheep.

**I am the good shepherd, and know my sheep, and am known of mine.**

**John 10:14**

Knowing your sheep means that you must know their names, where they live and where they work. Know about their health, friends, and school. Know when they are writing exams. Know their family, spouse and who they reside with. Know their financial situation and their occupation. Simply know all aspects of their lives. Know means know! It is only when you know more details about your sheep that you can help or advise them properly.

I once asked a pastor about one of his sheep. I asked, "Is he married?"

He answered, "I don't know."

"Where does he work?"

"I'm not sure." He answered.

"Did he come to church last week?"

"I didn't see him," he replied.

In a very large church, you may excuse such a question but in a small community church, the pastor has no excuse when he does not know many details about his sheep.

I recall one brother who belonged to a prominent church in my city. He joined another church, and after being a member of that ministry for a number of years, became a pastor himself. One day at a wedding he happened to meet his former senior pastor. His senior pastor said to him, "Brother 'X', it is a long time since I saw you."

"Did you come to church last Sunday?" the senior pastor asked.

Brother 'X' (who had now become a pastor in another church) smiled and said, "No pastor I didn't."

This senior pastor did not know that this brother had long since stopped coming to his church. He did not know that this gentleman had even become a pastor in another ministry. How sad!

Jesus said a good pastor knows his sheep. If God gives you twenty people to look after, make sure you know *all about them*. Do not let any of them slip out of your hands. Jesus kept saying, "Those that thou gavest me I have kept, and none of them is lost." (John 17:12). It is important to have many junior pastors and shepherds to work with the senior pastor so that none of the sheep get lost. **God will hold us accountable for every single sheep that is lost.** Keep the sheep that God has given to you.

### 6. A good shepherd is known.

A good shepherd "opens up" his life to the sheep so that they can know about him. The sheep are interested in the shepherd's life. Do not be a mystery figure to your sheep. Let them know how real you are and how you experience the same problems and temptations they do.

### 7. A good shepherd keeps the church family together.

The sheep of a good pastor are kept together under his "wings". **One of the cardinal features of the pastoral calling is the ability to keep people together through the years.**

The longer a group of people stay together the more the people step on each other's toes. The conflicts of a family begin to rise. Brothers turn against brothers and sisters against sisters. But it is a good pastor who keeps everybody together. The pastoral gift keeps employers in the same church with employees. The anointing on the shepherd is able to keep the old in the same room with the young. It keeps the married flowing with the unmarried.

As the church grows, you will even have enemies worshipping together under the same roof. It is the art of shepherding that will keep debtors and creditors within the same fold and prevent them from tearing each other apart.

> **But he that is an hireling, and not the shepherd, whose own the sheep are not, seeth the wolf coming, and leaveth the sheep, and fleeth: and the wolf catcheth them, and SCATTERETH THE SHEEP.**
>
> **John 10:12**

**8.    A good pastor notices the problems of his sheep.**

> **But he that is an hireling, and not a shepherd, whose own the sheep are not, SEETH THE WOLF COMING...**
>
> **John 10:12**

The Scripture tells us that the good shepherd can see the wolf coming. He sees the problems of his people and is concerned. He knows when they are doing exams. He knows when they are having marital problems.

He knows when their businesses' are going through "tough times". When a sheep fails his exams or loses a loved one, a wolf of discouragement and frustration is soon to come. **A good shepherd must be able to see the wolf and move into action.**

The bad shepherd sees the wolves and says, "That's your problem!" The good pastor will always stay with his sheep in their time of trouble.

## 9.  A good pastor delivers his sheep from captivity.

**...and the wolf catcheth them, and scattereth the sheep.**

**John 10:12**

Most of the members of a bad pastor are backslidden and in captivity. Shepherds, rise up and pray for your sheep! Minister to their needs. Apart from preaching, pray for their deliverance from witchcraft, demons and diseases. People love to be prayed for by their pastor. Pray for them, and anoint them with oil. They need this encouragement and ministration.

## 10.  A good shepherd wants to have more sheep.

A hireling is just around for a while, but a true shepherd is like the owner of the sheep. He is interested in them and he wants more. Every sheep owner wants to have more sheep because that makes him richer, naturally speaking. Yet, the servant or slave in the farm does not care whether there are more or fewer sheep because he is not the shepherd, he is the hireling.

**And other sheep I have... THEM ALSO I MUST BRING...**

**John 10:16**

The true pastor is always concerned about bringing in more sheep. That is why Jesus said, "Them also I must bring."

## 11.  A good pastor loves the sheep and not the money.

**But he that is an hireling, and NOT THE SHEPHERD...**

**John 10:12**

A true pastor does not work for money. He is interested in the salvation of souls and the growth of the church. **A bad pastor looks forward to some form of physical gain. His input is tied to that which he can get.** He is not concerned about the problems of his sheep. Anyone who cannot do pastoral work voluntarily, without being paid, is not genuine.

## 12. A good shepherd gives his life.

**I am the good shepherd: the good shepherd giveth his life for the sheep.**

**John 10:11**

A good shepherd sacrifices his time for the sheep. The bad shepherd is only prepared to give two hours of his time on Sundays. He always wants to get away from the crowd.

If a woman desires to be a good wife, she must give herself fully to her husband. If you want to be a good doctor, you must give yourself fully to medicine. **If you want to be a good shepherd, you must give your life and your time to the high calling of the pastoral office.** It is worth it at the end of the day.

Decide to be a good shepherd from today. You do not have to be paid to be a good pastor. In fact, many of the best pastors in the world are lay pastors!

## Chapter 14

# How to Become a Full-Time Shepherd

**I** started ministry as a lay shepherd. The idea of full-time ministry came up much later. I started my church as a medical student and thus found myself pastoring while at the same time practicing medicine. Later on, I went into business and combined business activities with pastoral work. At the end of 1990, the Lord told me to leave everything I was doing and enter into full-time ministry. It was not an easy decision for me.

There are many people who are in full-time ministry who should not really be there. There are many people, whom I believe should find secular jobs! How can a church with sixty members sustain four pastors and their families? Yet, this is the case for many ministries. Success in the ministry requires both power and wisdom.

> **But unto them which are called, both Jews and Greeks, Christ the power of God, and the wisdom of God.**
> **1 Corinthians 1:24**

There are many people whose ministries are frustrated because they entered full-time ministry too quickly. In this chapter, I want to share with you a few steps that I believe will give guidance when it comes to entering full-time ministry.

I am including this chapter because there are many people who will start out as lay shepherds and end up in full-time ministry. It is important to know when and how to make this great transition. I believe in full-time ministry! I consider it to be a privilege to be a full-time minister. I have always loved the ministry and thank God that I can now serve him with one hundred percent of my time.

If I had entered full-time ministry, even one year earlier than I did, the results might have been very different. What I am presenting in this chapter are not hard and fast rules about the ministry, they are just guiding principles of wisdom to help you into full-time ministry. There are five fundamental pre-conditions I believe you must fulfil before you enter into full-time ministry.

## Five Pre-conditions for Full-time Ministry

**1.  You must have a special call to sacrifice your Isaac.**

> **And it came to pass after these things, that God did tempt Abraham, and said unto him, Abraham: and he said, Behold, here I am.And he said, Take now thy son, thine only son Isaac, whom thou lovest, and get thee into the land of Moriah; and offer him there for a burnt offering upon one of the mountains which I will tell thee of.**

> **And Abraham rose up early in the morning, and saddled his ass, and took two of his young men with him, and Isaac his son, and clave the wood for the burnt offering, and rose up, and went unto the place of which God had told him.**

> **Then on the third day Abraham lifted up his eyes, and saw the place afar off.  And Abraham said unto his young men, Abide ye here with the ass; and I and the lad will go yonder and worship, and come again to you.**

> **And Abraham took the wood of the burnt offering, and laid it upon Isaac his son; and he took the fire in his hand, and a knife; and they went both of them together.**

> **And Isaac spake unto Abraham his father, and said, My father: and he said, Here am I, my son.  And he said, Behold the fire and the wood: but where is the lamb for a burnt offering?**

> **And Abraham said, My son, God will provide himself a lamb for a burnt offering: so they went both of them together.**

> **And they came to the place which God had told him of; and Abraham built an altar there, and laid the wood**

**in order, and bound Isaac his son, and laid him on the altar upon the wood.**

**And Abraham stretched forth his hand, and took the knife to slay his son.**

**And the angel of the Lord called unto him out of heaven, and said, Abraham, Abraham: and he said, Here am I.**

**And he said, Lay not thine hand upon the lad, neither do thou any thing unto him: for now I know that thou fearest God, seeing thou hast not withheld thy son, thine only son from me.**

**Genesis 22:1-12**

In this story, God spoke to Abraham and asked him to give up his most treasured possession – his son. **Some people have the mistaken view that God asks everyone to sacrifice their "Isaac".** God did not ask Joseph to sacrifice his sons. Neither did He ask Jacob or Isaac to sacrifice their sons. **King David was a man after God's own heart, but God did not ask David to sacrifice his son.**

God deals with everyone differently! What God requires of me may be different from what God will require of you. God has asked me for my profession. Perhaps God will not ask you for your profession. **I believe that before you enter full-time ministry, you must have a definite call to give up your treasured secular job. This is different from the call to follow God.**

God spoke to Abraham and directed him on many occasions. That was a call to follow and Abraham was faithful to follow the Lord each time.

**Now the Lord had said unto Abram, Get thee out of thy country, and from thy kindred, and from thy father's house, unto a land that I will shew thee:**

**Genesis 12:1**

**Arise, walk through the land in the length of it and in the breadth of it; for I will give it unto thee. Then Abram removed his tent, and came and dwelt in the**

**plain of Mamre, which is in Hebron, and built there an altar unto the Lord.**

**Genesis 13:17, 18**

Then came the special call to give up Isaac! God may call you to follow Him. But that call to give up Isaac may never come! It is an entirely different thing. Everyone must obey God on an individual basis. I am not you and you are not me! What has worked for me may not work for you. What works for you may not work for me! If God is in it, it will work and there will be a blessing. So make sure that you have a definite call to give up your Isaac before you do so.

2.   **You must demonstrate faithfulness in handling a few things.**

The Bible teaches clearly that he that is faithful with little will be faithful with much.

> **He that is faithful in that which is least is faithful also in much: and he that is unjust in the least is unjust also in much. If therefore ye have not been faithful in the unrighteous mammon, who will commit to your trust the true riches? And if ye have not been faithful in that which is another man's, who shall give you that which is your own?**

**Luke 16:10-12**

If somebody is not faithful with a little responsibility, how will he be faithful when he is in full-time ministry? Many people are not doing well in full-time ministry because they did not do well as lay people.

I worked for the Lord for years without supervision! I did not need anybody to tell me to get up to pray or to study my Bible! I was faithful with Scripture Union fellowships whilst I was in secondary school. I was faithful as an organist in Calvary Road Incorporated (a Christian singing group). I was faithful as a drummer and pianist for Victory Church in London. I was faithful with the fellowships in the university. It never once crossed my mind that I should be paid. No one ever told me what to do – I just did what I thought was right. And God blessed it!

### 3.  A ministry that needs a full-time pastor.

Not every ministry needs a full-time pastor. Most of our churches are pastored by unpaid pastors.  Jesus pays them directly!

If there are only twenty-five people in the church, it is obvious that it cannot sustain a full-time minister.  Many of the church members secretly ask, "What does the full-time pastor do all day?"

Many people think that the pastor sleeps from morning to evening. The fact is that there isn't much to do with a congregation of thirty.  The ministry has to develop to the point where it needs a full-time worker.  The other reality that you have to face is that, most of the members are at work during the day and only become available during the evenings.

Pastors are not bankers, accountants or pharmacists.  They are shepherds who are supposed to look after sheep.  The working hours are different for different professions!  **I do not work from nine to five everyday because I am not an accountant, I am a pastor!  When the sheep become available in the evenings I become very active.**

There are some pastors who have become idle and lazy as they wait for Sunday when they can deliver their next sermon.

> **For we hear that there are some which walk among you disorderly, WORKING NOT AT ALL...**
> **2 Thessalonians 3:11**

Let us be honest!  Let us be realistic!  Does your church need so many full-time pastors?  Does it need even one full-time pastor?  Can the income of the church sustain the pastor and his family?  Can the pastor not find a secular job to do?  Pastors are frustrated and fearful because they are not sure whether they will be able to survive until the next month. Let that frustration die today! **Get a job and pastor the church on the side until it grows and demands your full attention!**

The Swiss missionaries who were sent to Ghana many years ago were sent as *self-sustaining ministers*. They came equipped with skills that would enable them to work in Africa as they did their ministry work. That is a good example to follow. We need self-sustaining ministers today more than ever before. Most churches cannot bear the burden of maintaining so many full-time pastors.

I purposely keep my ministry staff as small as possible. I want to pay people properly. I do not want idle and discontented people around me. **Idleness leads to laziness and laziness leads to discontentment and discontentment leads to disloyalty.**

**And withal they learn to be idle, wandering about from house to house; and not only idle, but tattlers also and busybodies, speaking things which they ought not.**

**1 Timothy 5:13**

### 4. A death to the love of silver

**He that loveth silver shall not be satisfied with silver; nor he that loveth abundance with increase: this is also vanity.**

**Ecclesiastes 5:10**

*The ministry is not an alternative source of employment for anyone.* It was never intended to be! It is a special job that God gives to those whom He has called. **As the church becomes larger, it often deteriorates into a source of employment for the unemployed.** This attracts many people who have no calling at all. What then happens to the church? It becomes full of seekers of wealth and lovers of silver. These pastors who are seeking for gold, end up always fighting for better salaries and conditions of service.

Many pastors see the ministry as a way to travel around the world and to drive nice cars. I did not enter the ministry in order to drive a nice car. I did not come into the ministry because I wanted to have the nice things of this world. Actually, coming into full-time ministry was, for me, the end of all hopes of ever having the nice things of this world.

**I AM CRUCIFIED WITH CHRIST: NEVERTHE-LESS I LIVE; yet not I, but Christ liveth in me: and the life which I now live in the flesh I live by the faith of the Son of God, who loved me, and gave himself for me. I do not frustrate the grace of God: for if righteousness come by the law, then Christ is dead in vain.**

**Galatians 2:20, 21**

A minister who is going to serve God properly must have died to the love for silver and gold. Why is this? The Bible teaches that those that love silver are never satisfied with silver. The more you give them, the more they want. Why is it that many rich people in this world are also thieves?

Is it because they are poor? Is it because they are in need? Certainly not! It is because of the greed for more and more and more!

I have found that you cannot satisfy people with more and more money. From experience, whenever I have felt under pressure to raise salaries, I have often discovered that, that does not solve the root of the problem!

Senior pastors, if you feel under pressure to raise salaries and give more and more benefits, you will discover that the problem never goes away. **I believe that full-time ministers must be people who just want to serve the Lord at heart.** This does not mean that people will be poor but it means that the heart is not craving endlessly after more and more.

Soon the church becomes unionized with the workers against the management, and the management against the workers! The "management" are often the senior pastors who make decisions and the "workers" are the other pastors and workers who are not involved in the decision-making. **There is much bitterness, petty jealousy and bickering amongst full-time staff of many churches.**

I would rather have one or two workers with peace than to have a hundred discontented full-time staff.

### 5. A total surrender for all possibilities

As you enter into full-time ministry you must be open for whatever the future will bring. You may be rich or you may be poor. You may have abundance or you may live in the "want of all things". Are you ready for anything?

**Verily, verily, I say unto thee, When thou wast young, thou girdedst thyself, and walkedst whither thou wouldest: but when thou shalt be old, thou shalt stretch forth thy hands, and another shall gird thee, and carry thee whither thou wouldest not. This spake he, signifying by what death he should glorify God. And when he had spoken this, he saith unto him, Follow me.**

**John 21:18, 19**

Jesus told Peter to be ready for anything. Be ready to be carried anywhere. It will no longer be your will, but God's will. You are not the commander, you are just one of God's workers. One of the reasons why I am in the ministry is because I have no choice!

**...woe is unto me, if I preach not the gospel!**
**1 Corinthians 9:16**

God has told me to do it, so I just have to do it. I must obey Him at all costs. I refuse to listen to the detractors, faultfinders, analysts and commentators who talk about me all the time. I have no time for empty chatter. I prefer to hear my dogs barking in the morning than to listen to hateful accusations! I must continue doing what God has called me to do. Some people love me for what I do and others hate me. I thank God for them all. But I press on for the mark of the prize of the high calling.

I am totally surrendered to fulfilling the call of God upon my life, so help me God!